Essays on Indian Philosophy

Essays on Indian Philosophy

SHRI KRISHNA SAKSENA

UNIVERSITY OF HAWAII PRESS
HONOLULU
1970

Library of Congress Catalog Card Number 78-114209
Standard Book Number 87022-726-2

Printed in the United States of America

Contents

Acknowledgments

The author wishes to make the following acknowledgments for permission to reprint previously published essays:

"The Story of Indian Philosophy," in *A History of Philosophical Systems*, edited by Vergilius Ferm. New York: The Philosophical Library, 1950.

"Basic Tenets of Indian Philosophy," previously published as "Are There Any Basic Tenets of Indian Philosophy?" in *The Philosophical Quarterly*.

"Testimony in Indian Philosophy," previously published as "Authority in Indian Philosophy," in *Philosophy East and West*, vol. 1, no. 3 (October 1951).

"Hinduism," in *Studium Generale*, no. 10 (1962).

"The Jain Religion," previously published as "Jainism," in *Religion in the Twentieth Century*, edited by Vergilius Ferm. New York: The Philosophical Library, 1948.

"Autobiography of a Yogi," in *Philosophy East and West*, vol. 1, no. 2 (July 1951).

"Jainism," © 1969, Encyclopaedia Britannica, Inc.

"Svapramanatva and Svaprakasatva: An Inconsistency in Kumārila's Philosophy," in *Review of Philosophy and Religion*.

"The Nature of Buddhi according to Sānkhya-Yoga," in *The Philosophical Quarterly*.

"The Individual in Social Thought and Practice in India," in *Status of the Individual in East and West*, Honolulu: University of Hawaii Press, 1968; also in *The Indian Mind*, Honolulu: East-West Center Press, 1967.

"Professor Zaehner and the Comparison of Religions," in *Algemeen Nederlands Tijdschrift voor Wijsbegeerte en Phychologies*, May 1969.

"A Comparison between the Eastern and Western Portrait of Man in Our Time," was first published in German as "Ein Vergleich zwischen dem ostlichen und dem westlichen Menschenbild in unserer Zeit," in *Menschliche Existenz und moderne Velt* [Human Existence and Modern World] , edited and co-authored by Richard Schwarz. Berlin: Walter de Gruyer and Co., 1967.

Essays on Indian Philosophy

The Story of Indian Philosophy

Indian philosophy is perhaps the earliest recorded thought of man. Its four thousand years of history embracing the multitudinous phases of intense enquiry cannot possibly be done justice in this chapter. Only a bird's-eye view of this vast panorama is possible in the following survey.

THE VEDAS

The *Vedas* (2500-2000 B. C.), which embody divine truths, are believed to have been revealed to the super-consciousness of the seers. They represent the fountainhead of Hindu philosophical thought. Each of the four *Vedas, Rig-Veda, Yajur-Veda, Sāma-Veda* and *Atharva-Veda,* has three main divisions: the *Samhitās* (sacred texts), the *Brāhmaṇas* (commentaries) and the *Āraṇyakas* (forest books). The *Rig-Veda Samhitā* is the oldest record of Hindu philosophical thought.

To begin with, man looks outside. His first thoughts therefore relate to the sequence of natural phenomena in which he sees the causes of vicissitudes of his everyday life. The early *mantras* (hymns), thus, contain an element of nature worship, in which the various powers of nature such as fire (Agni) and wind (Vāyu), which influence human life, are personified as gods, whom it is a man's duty to propitiate. Varuṇa and Indra are the chief among them, the former being conceived as a symbol of omniscience and righteousness. The gods being righteous are believed to uphold *Rta,* or the physical and moral order in the universe. The relationship of man to gods who are conceived as originating and sustaining the world is one of utter dependence. Man, it is maintained, must lead a righteous life to please the gods who are good. In Vedic religious thought the unreality of the universe is never suggested. In fact, worldly prosperity and the joys of everyday life are constantly stressed. Transmigration is not directly referred to though the soul is conceived as immortal.

In later hymns and the *Brāhmaṇas,* the development of thought takes three distinct lines: monotheism, monism, and ritualism. Identity in the conception of different gods suggests monotheism. A supreme God is not yet conceived, however, an attempt is made to discover a common power behind all the gods. God, or *Prajāpati,* is such a power. The monistic tendency traces the world not to a creator but to a single primal cause, diversifying itself into the universe, which anticipating the later Upaniṣadic Absolute is described as *Tat Ekam,* or That One. Here, therefore, the focus of attention turns from the concrete and the external to the abstract and the internal, which is later followed up in the *Upaniṣads.*

Ritualism, representing the effort to gain the favor of the gods through sacrificial gifts, culminates in the *Brāhmaṇas.* It is just another way of looking at the concept of *Rta,* according to which a correct sacrifice inexorably brings its own good result.

THE UPANIṢADS

Upaniṣads (700-600 B. C.) literally means "secret teaching." Forming the concluding part of the *Vedas,* they are also called the *Vedānta* and *Āraṇyakas*—or the forest books. They mark a distinct step beyond the *Brāhmaṇas.* Of the major *Upaniṣads,* about ten are the most celebrated, the *Brihadāraṇyaka* and the *Chāndogya* being the most important among them. Their exalted idealism and lofty teachings have had a lasting influence upon the Indian mind. Much of the subsequent Indian philosophy, in one way or another, draws inspiration from the *Upaniṣads.*

In the *Upaniṣads* the stress is, not on the traditional performance of action *(Karma-mārga),* but on the knowledge of the ultimate truth as a means to the final liberation of man *(Jñāna-mārga).* Apart from this shift in emphasis, the *Upaniṣads* inaugurate a new era of "looking within" for the reality of the universe as opposed to the Vedic perception of the *Puruṣa* as a macrocosmic reality.

Thought here is devoted chiefly to the concept of the *Ātman* and the *Brāhmaṇ.* The quest after *Brāhmaṇ* as the all-pervasive spirit springs from the desire to discover a Supreme Controller of man and nature. By progressive elimination, this ultimate reality is found by the *Upaniṣads* to be none other than man's own Self, which is also the *Brāhmaṇ.* This alone is real. But the problem is: If the *Ātman* alone is real, what happens to the reality of the external world? Though the universe is a reality, say the *Upaniṣads,* the real in it is the *Ātman* alone. The most pervading thought is that the *Ātman* is the only reality, though in places we also find the pantheistic thought which identifies the universe with the *Brāhmaṇ* and the theistic thought which looks upon the *Brāhmaṇ* as the Lord of the Universe.

The *Ātman* is characterized as transcendental and beyond the reach of the senses and the intellect. It is a pure, subject-object-less consciousness. Sometimes it is identified with *Brāhmaṇ*, as in the sayings, *That thou art (tat tvam asi)* and *I am Brāhmaṇ (aham brāhma asmi)*. But the meaning is that the *Ātman* alone underlies man and nature and not that there are two realities which are one. Demonstrating that it is *not this, not this (neti, neti)*, the indescribability of the *Brāhmaṇ* is also stressed.

Next, after the doctrine of the *Ātman* and its realization, is the doctrine of transmigration. The significance of this doctrine is that it points to desire and not to *Karma* as the cause of rebirth. *Karma* only forms the connecting link between desire and rebirth, for "whatever a man desires he wills, and whatever he wills he acts." Desire is annihilated by Self-knowledge. *Mokṣa* (emancipation) is the state of infiniteness which a man attains when he realizes his own Self. Transmigration naturally ceases for such a knowing man. He transcends limits and is happy, for the infinite is bliss, just as the finite is pain. Emancipation is not the attainment of something that is not: it is only the true knowledge of the Self that ever is.

THE EPICS AND THE BHAGAVAD-GĪTĀ

A few centuries of thought, separating the Vedic period from the later systems, are embodied in the epic of the *Mahābhārata* containing the *Bhagavad-Gītā* of the Lord Krishna and some minor *Upaniṣads*. The continuation of Vedic monotheism, the emergence of two new creeds *(Śaivism* and *Vaiśnavism* glorifying the Vedic deities of *Śiva* and *Vishnu* respectively), the concept of *Dharma* as predominantly ritualistic, and various other notions of *Bhakti* (devotion) and *Prasāda* (divine grace) are the chief philosophical features of this period. During this period the concepts of *Karma* and *Mokṣa* were refined. The *Gītā*, second only to the *Upaniṣads* in philosophical importance, advocates *Niṣkāma-karma*, or performance of duty without thought of consequences. According to the *Gītā*, one's own duty *(Sva-dharma)* is relative to one's social status. Every duty is as good as every other; only it is to be done in a spirit of non-attachment *(Karma-yoga)*. Duty in the *Gītā*, however, is conceived in absolutist as well as in theistic terms; the latter forms the basis of *Bhakti-yoga,* or dedication of all work to the Lord.

THE CHĀRVĀKA

This heterogeneous material perhaps could not long remain without systematization, hence, the transition to systems. First comes the *Chārvāka,* or the *Lokāyata,* that is, the commonsense philosophy restricted to the world of common experience. This is regarded as one of the heterodox or non-Vedic systems as it believes neither in revelation nor in the authority of the *Vedas.* Things, it maintains, have no transcendental essence: they are what they appear to be. Only the perceived elements—earth, water, fire, and air—are real. Supersensible entities, like God, soul, and the divine origin of the *Vedas* are ridiculed. Perception being the only source of knowledge, life is to be taken as it is, a mixture of pain and pleasure. It is vain to strive after a painless existence: Wisdom is maximizing the balance of pleasure over pain. Yet the system does not recommend purely animalistic living. It may be taken as an earlier counterpart to Western Epicureanism.

JAINISM

Another non-Vedic religion is Jainism. Its name is derived from the word *Jin,* meaning the conquest of life's suffering. It is older than Hinduism or Buddhism. Its founder was Riṣabha, the first *Tirthānkara,* or perfect soul (Lord Mahavīra being the last of the series of *Tirthānkaras).* Its two well-known sects are the *Śvetāmbaras* (the white-clad) and the *Digāmbaras* (the sky-clad). Their central philosophy, however, is the same.

Jain metaphysics is both dualistic and pluralistic. The animate and inanimate, or the *Jīva* and *Ajīva,* are both treated as eternal, independent, and numberless. The *Jīva,* meaning only the individual soul and not the supreme Self of the *Upaniṣads,* is always mixed up with matter except when liberated. It may be mobile or immobile as in stones, but *Cetana* (consciousness) is its chief quality. It is by nature ever active to perfect itself: the *Tirthānkaras* are these perfected souls. Most of the functions of God are attributed to the *Jīva's* potential power. It may be *Mukta* (liberated) or *Baddha* (in bondage). The former has the usual characteristics of perfect knowledge, power, and bliss.

The *Ajīvas* are five in number—*Pudgala*, or Matter; *Ākāṣa*, or Space; *Kāla*, or Time; *Dharma*, or Movement; and *Adharma*, or Rest—the last two being peculiar to Jainism.

Karma is described as the soul-energy that links the soul with the body. The Law of Karma is said to operate inexorably. Normally, every soul is mixed up with matter through *Karma:* this is bondage. Liberation consists in finally extinguishing *Karma*. Therein lies the perfection of man. Jainism is, in fact, the religion of the Perfect Man. No more perfect or higher being like God is visualized for the origination or maintenance of the universe, hence, the atheistic touch in the system. To attain this spiritual perfection, non-injury to all life is recommended. *Ahimsā*, the supreme ethical principle, is not mere non-injury but also positive love for all. Right faith *(Samyag Darshan)* and right knowledge *(Samyag Jyāna)* are basic to right conduct *(Samyag Cāritra)*. The ideal conceived is the supreme happiness of all creatures.

Jain logic gives us the distinctive theory of the manyness of reality and the difference of viewpoints, known as the *Anekānta-vāda*. Every proposition is held to be only partially real or unreal or both real and unreal from different points of view. Jain logic, therefore, prefixes propositions with may be, or *Syad*. Knowledge is classified into five kinds: *Mati*, or perceptual knowledge; *Śruti*, or scriptural; *Avadhi*, or clairvoyant; *Manahprayāya*, or telepathic; and *Kevala Jyāna*, or absolute knowledge.

BUDDHISM

Buddhism, founded by Lord Buddha (563 B.C.), is the revolt of reason against the transcendentalism of the *Upaniṣads* and the excessive ritualism of the Vedic age. Early Buddhism was a gospel of hope though later it took a negative turn. Through self-effort and concrete moral goodness *(Dharma)* the individual is advised to realize his spiritual nature and annihilate suffering. Buddhism, as it later asserted itself, can be summed up as follows:

> Life is suffering. Suffering has a cause. This cause can be eliminated, and there is a way or *Mārga* to the elimination of suffering. The cause of suffering is ignorance *(Avidyā)*, which consists in not knowing the nature of the Self as a composite of body *(Rūpa)* and mind *(Nāma)* and as ever changing. All things including the Self are just aggregates *(Saṃghata)*. Ignorance causes cravings *(Tṛṣnā)* which, being unsatisfied, cause rebirth. In *Nirvāṇa*, (emancipation), the *Nāma-rūpa* is completely annihilated. *Nirvāṇa*, or a state of serene composure, comes to the worthy *(Arhan)*,

who have broken through the cycle of birth and death *(Saṃsāra)* by following the eight-fold path of discipline which stresses right conduct *(Śila)*, right knowledge *(Prajnā)*, and right concentration *(Samādhī)*.

The two schools, *Hīnayāna* (small wheel) and *Mahāyāna* (large wheel), into which Buddhism gradually split itself both entertain the theory of momentariness *(Kṣana-bhangvāda)*. At every moment, everything is changing into something else, and identity is only an illusion. Even the Self is defined as a continuous succession of ideas. Facts of memory and moral responsibility can be explained by similarity which the different appearances of the Self bear to one another. External objects are, therefore, a series *(Santāna)* of unique particulars. Universals are dismissed as ideal superimpositions upon the object. This refusal to admit unity and universality as real is in direct opposition to Jainism.

Mahāyāna Buddhism is represented by two idealistic schools—the *Yogācāras* and the *Mādhyamikas*. The *Yogācāras* whose *Vijnāna-vāda* (theory of the sole reality of ideas) maintains that knowledge points to no objects beyond itself and explains that an object (including the Self) is a mere series of ideas resembles closely the modern subjective idealists. The *Mādhyamikas*, who deny both the external objects and the Self, are like the modern nihilists. The latter school is also called the *Śūnyavāda*, or the doctrine of the void, which, however, does grant a sort of reality to the subject and object and does seem to suggest that the ultimate reality is called *Śūnya* because it is incomprehensible and not because it is non-existent.

In spite of common ethical practice, the ethical teaching of the two schools differs in some respects. While the Hīnayāna scheme of individual perfection is virtually the same as in canonical Buddhism, Mahāyāna Buddhism maintains that the ideal man or the *Bodhisattva* attains his own perfection through social channels.

THE SIX SYSTEMS

While later Indian thought seems to diverge from the original source and to diversify itself into a number of conflicting systems, perhaps, it would not be correct to regard them as independent schools of thought. They are more in the nature of an elaboration of different aspects of the same thought. The six well-known systems of Indian philosophy are an amplification of the monistic, the dualistic, and the pluralistic trends of the traditional Hindu thought. We shall briefly note them in pairs.

THE NYĀYA-VAIŚEṢIKA

The two systems of the *Nyāya* and the *Vaiśeṣika* are generally summarized together. Their basic books are the *Vaiśeṣika Sūtras* of Kaṇāda with the glossary by Prasasta Pāda and the *Nyāya Sūtras* of Gautama with the commentary of Vātsyāyna. Gangesa in A.D. 1200 gave the system its prevailing logical character.

This system is both realistic and pluralistic. It acknowledges the external world as independently real and no other substances *(Dravyas)*—earth, water, air, fire, *akāṣa,* space, time, self, and *manas* —as ultimately real. Separate reality of universals *(Sāmānya)* of qualities (such as odor, sound, knowledge, *dharma, adharma, karma), Abhāva* (non-existence), and *Samavāya* (a relation of one-sided dependence) are also fully recognized. The physical universe is conceived as consisting of numberless atoms (inferred from the divisibility of objects) and the three all-pervading entities, *akāsa,* space, and time. Every atom is regarded as unique *(Visesa). Nyāya-Vaiśeṣika* believes in the causal theory of origination *(Ārmabha-vāda),* that is, atomic aggregation can produce something new and distinct. It does not believe in the preexistence of the effect in the cause *(Asatkāryavāda)* as in the *Sānkhya-Yoga* system.

God is conceived only as an efficient cause or the Being who manipulated the external atoms into creation. Individual selves vary in their past deeds, or *Karma.* The world serves the dual role of enabling the individual to reap the fruits of his *Karma* and also of freeing him from its shackles. The vast variety of the world is made to argue for God's infinite power and wisdom.

Reality of both Self and God is postulated on the basis of introspection and inference. The *Ātman,* or the individual Self, is an eternal spiritual principle although psychically featureless. Knowledge or consciousness appears only when certain external features cooperate with the Self through the medium of the *Manas,* or the mind. The Selves are many and fundamentally distinct.

Nyāya-Vaiśeṣika Epistemology

Nyāya-Vaiśeṣika epistemology is as realistic as its metaphysics. It lays down four *Pramānas* as the valid means of knowledge. They are: perception, inference, analogy, and authority. Perception reveals objects directly and inference, indirectly. Knowledge is true if it works in practical life; the pragmatic criterion, however, constitutes only a test and not the essence of truth which lies in correspondence. Even error has an objective basis. A rope exists; it only appears as something different in erroneous perception

(Anyathā-khyāti). Side by side with this realistic epistemology, a transcendental *(Alaukika)* form of perception which enables the Yogin to perceive atoms and moral merit *(Dharma)* is also recognized.

Mokṣa, or the ultimate end, is conceived as the transcendence of pleasure and pain on the part of the Self. This is achieved only after death. Liberation consists in realizing that the Self is neither the body nor the *Manas.* Right knowledge, detached living, and meditation upon the ultimate truth *(Yoga)* are prescribed as means to liberation.

THE SĀNKHYA-YOGA

The two systems of the *Sānkhya* and the *Yoga,* founded many centuries before Christ by Kapila and Pātaṇjali respectively, are dualistic in thought and recognize two independent, ultimate, and eternal principles, namely, the *Puruṣa* and the *Prakṛiti,* as the transcendental essences of the conscious and the unconscious in our everyday life. While the system is dualistic, in its concept of the *Puruṣa,* it is a bulwark of idealism. *Puruṣa* is regarded as pure spirit, inactive, and unchanging, while *Prakṛiti* is unconscious, active, and ever changing. The system, however, is not free from the difficulties of a satisfactory relationship between the two mutually exclusive and independent principles.

The ever changing, primordial *Prakṛiti,* which modifies itself into twenty-four evolutions of increasing grossness, along with the unchanging *Puruṣa* constitute the matrix of our universe. *Prakṛiti's* modifications are successively the *Mahat* (reason), *Buddhi* (mind), and *Ahankāra* (principle of individuation), from which are derived the five elements *(Tanmātras)* and the five gross elements (ether, air, light, water, and earth) which, in turn, give us the ten senses and the *Manas.* Evolution is regarded as *Prakṛiti's* self-modification for the sake of *Puruṣa.* The evolutions of the *Prakṛiti* are regarded as potentially present in the cause, for nothing new can really be produced. This theory of the potential presence of the effect in the cause is known as *Satkāryavāda.* Though the system recognizes just one ultimate spiritual principle, it somehow provides for many selves, or individual *Jīvas,* also. The *Jīvas* are the results of the *Puruṣa's* contact with *Ahankāra* and the *Ling-śarīra,* or the subtle body. It is the *Jīva* that needs liberation from suffering. The *Puruṣa,* linked only temporarily with *Prakṛiti,* is ever free. Knowledge involves the *Jīva,* the object, and the activity of the internal organ *(Antah-karaṇa)* which links the illumining *Puruṣa* with the object. Thus objects are only mediately known. Highest knowledge, called *Viveka-jñāna,* is intuitive and consists in a clear discrimination of the *Puruṣa* from the *Prakṛiti.*

Yoga here means the discipline required for the restoration of the original and free status of the individual Self, and *Viyoga,* or separation of the *Jīva* from the true Self, is regarded as the prime cause of suffering.

To the *Sānkhya* aim of discrimination *(Viveka)* between *Puruṣa* and *Prakṛiti,* the *Yoga* adds an eight-fold psycho-physical discipline for the reattainment of the *Puruṣa's* originally pure nature (experienced in the state of *Asamprajnāta Samādhi).* This means complete transcendence of life's suffering whether psychological *(Ādhyātmika),* environmental *(Ādhibhautika),* or supernatural *(Ādhidaivika).*

God is rejected on grounds of logic and life's sufferings, though *Yoga* admits Him as an aid to spiritual realization. In short, *Sānkhya-Yoga* is an exalted idealism without theistic implications wherein the wonderful harmony of the *Puruṣa* and the *Prakṛiti* are supposed to discharge the functions of God.

The Mīmāmsā

Mīmāmsā, literally meaning systematic investigation, stresses reflection, or *Vicāra.* The *Pūrva* and the *Uttar Mīmāmsā* are based upon the *Brāhmaṇas* and the *Upaniṣads* respectively. The earliest literature of the *Pūrva Mīmāmsā* is known as Jaimini's *Sūtra* (about 300-200 B.C.) and has been interpreted differently by Kumārila Bhatt and Prabhākar Misra. *Mīmāmsā* believes in plurality of souls and material ultimates and is both pluralistic and realistic.

The *Mīmāmsā* envisages a vague kind of modified pluralism inasmuch as Reality is described as "identity in difference." Five categories, substance, quality, action, universals, and non-existence, are admitted. The Self is regarded as all-pervading and eternal. Two kinds of universals, abstract and concrete, are recognized. Otherwise, the categories are generally conceived in the *Nyāya-Vaiśeṣika* fashion.

Mīmāmsā has some notable contributions to make in the field of epistemology. The Self is supposed to be known in all knowledge although only as an object. For instance, in "I see a table" both the "I-notion" and the "table-notion" are apprehended. Knowledge is a changing activity of the Self, which, in knowing, manifests itself as well as the object. Objects are known directly and the Self, indirectly. According to *Mīmāmsā* epistemology, all knowledge is intrinsically valid; all error is either due to outside interference in the apparatus of knowing or due to conflict with another bit of knowledge. Prabhākara attributes error to some omission *(Akhyāti)* and Kumārila to commission *(Khyāti).*

According to *Mīmāmsā,* mere knowledge *(Jyāna)* does not lead to *Mokṣa* without detached performance of duty *(Karma).* The *Vedas,* it is maintained, determine *Dharma* (religious duties). *Sanyāsa,* or retirement from life, is not prescribed; performance of Vedic rites is deemed capable of achieving the cherished goal. In short, the *Mīmāmsā* discipline consists in doing the obligatory deeds and avoiding the prohibited ones which are the direct cause of birth and suffering.

The Vedānta (Absolutistic)

The *Uttar Mīmāmsā,* more popularly known as the *Vedānta,* is the *Upaniṣads* systematized and represents the cream of Indian thought. The *Upaniṣads,* the *Bhagavad-Gītā,* and the *Sūtras* of *Bādarayaṇa* form the base of the *Vedānta.* It may be classified as absolutistic, representing the Ultimate Reality as an impersonal principle, and theistic, representing the Ultimate Reality as a personal God. The absolutistic *Advaita* is represented by Śankara while the theistic type is represented by Rāmānuja and Mādhva.

Sankara (A.D. 788-820) maintained that the *Upaniṣads* really teach unity, their inclusion of diversity being only expository. The real, he held, is one, eternal, and of the essence of pure *Cit,* called the *Brahman.* The Absolute is changeless. The change attributed to the *Brahman* and the world is only apparent. Nothing else is. Yet the *Brahman* is not always realized as such. Thus, something other than the *Brahman* also is; the world also appears, but it is illusory as it is neither real nor unreal. It is of the nature of the "serpent in the rope," which is neither existent nor non-existent. The Absolute appears as the world just as the rope appears as a serpent. Thus the world has another kind of reality though not the Absolute Reality. The Absolute appears not only as the world but also as the individual Self. This is due to the delimiting adjuncts of the Self like the internal organ *(Antah-karaṇa).* The true Self is to be seen shorn of its conditionings. Just as one light appears to be different through different shades, even so the individual Self, when seen *sub specie aeternitatis,* is *Brahman* itself. Thus *Brahman* alone appears both as the objective universe and as the individual Self.

The Māyā

The appearance of the world and the plurality of the individual selves, if these are appearances, have to be adequately explained.

This is done by the concept of *Māyā*, or the principle of nescience. The existence of *Avidyā* in ourselves cannot be denied. As *Avidyā* dissolves and true *Vidyā*, or the knowledge of the *Brahman*, dawns, the *Brahman* is more and more revealed. On complete realization of true knowledge, nothing remains but the *Brahman*. Not only is the world and the plurality of the Selves destroyed, but along with it *Avidyā* also disappears. *Māyā* also is both real and unreal, that is, it is practically real but ultimately unreal. That is why it is called *Anirvacanīya*, or indescribable. This admission of the principle of *Māyā* in *Advaita Vedānta* has evoked persistent objections from non-*Advaitic* systems, but the *Advaitists* have never regarded it as a vulnerable point in their metaphysics.

Advaita, however, is not subjectivism, for according to *Advaita* epistemology, all knowledge points to an object beyond it. Even error has an objective counterpart. The appearance of the snake in the rope is not real, but it is not wholly unreal either, or else it could not appear at all. Error is thus the apprehension of that which is neither being nor non-being, hence, it is inexpressible *Anirvacanīya*. Ultimate truth is not only coherent but also all-comprehensive. "All this, verily, is *Brahman*" *(sarvam khalvidam brahma)*. Man's ultimate aim is to know that he himself is *Brahman*. The ego is a blend of the Self and the non-Self. Any objectification of the Self is *Avidyā*, or the individual's share of *Māyā*. To know oneself as *Brahman* and as completely dissociated from the non-Self is true knowledge and man's complete emancipation.

VEDĀNTA-THEISTIC

As if by a natural rebound against the absolutism of Śankara, the theistic tendencies of *Śaivism* and *Vaiśnavism* tried to reassert themselves, and in the *Viśiṣtādvaita* of Rāmānuja (A.D. 1100) we find a powerful attempt to synthesize *Vaiśnavism* with *Vedānta*. The effort is embodied in Rāmānuja's commentaries on the *Vedānta-Sūtra* and the *Gītā*.

The world and the soul, says Rāmānuja, are to the *Brahman* what the body is to the soul. Neither can exist nor be conceived without Him *(Aprathak-siddhi)*. In the *Upaniṣads*, it is contended that all the three are distinct and eternal, though of unequal status and inseparably associated. The one *Brahman*, however, informs and sustains both Matter and Soul: hence monism *(Advaita)*. The embodied is one: the embodying, many: hence qualified monism *(Viśiṣtādvaita)*.

In theistic *Advaita*, *Prakṛiti*, *Jīva*, and God are conceived as important substances. Out of *Prakṛiti*, whose nature and evolution is conceived largely in the *Sāmkhya-Yoga* fashion, the world evolves under the guidance of God. But the world is an adjunct and not a transformation of Him. Though atomic, the *Jīva* can perceive far-off things because it possesses attributive intelligence *(Dharma-ghūta-jñāna,* also attributed to God). It is essentially sentient and self-revealing. The souls are intrinsically happy: only past deeds *(Karma)* compel them to transmigration and suffering. God is self-existent, all-knowing, and all-powerful. He is the sole unchanging cause of the universe.

Knowledge, it is maintained, always reveals a complex object, hence, the falsity of conceiving *Brahman* as *Nirguṇa,* or featureless. Knowledge is necessarily true, even erroneous apprehension being true as far as it goes.

The end of life is to attain the perfectly free and blissful world of *Nārāyana. Prapatti,* or complete self-surrender to Him, and *Bhakti,* or loving meditation based upon highest knowledge, are the means to it.

The Advaita

This doctrine, like *Viśistādvaita,* is theistic and identifies God with Nārāyan or Vishnu. But it is more explicity pluralistic inasmuch as individual souls and physical objects are both treated as distinct from one another. *Bheda,* or uniqueness, according to this system, is manifold. There is a difference between God and Soul, between the different Souls, between Soul and Matter, and between the discrete material objects. The majesty of God is taken as the basis of His being distinct from the world, which He completely controls. God is the only independent entity recognized: hence, It is no ordinary pluralism. He is conceived as the all-controlling personality. The evolution of *Prakṛiti,* conceived as the ultimate source of the physical world, is explained through the theory of *Sadāsat-kārya-vāda*—that before its production, the effect is both existent and non-existent in the cause.

Knowledge, it is maintained, is due to a transformation of the internal organ *(Manas)* and not of the Self. All knowledge, even erroneous knowledge, points to an object beyond itself. Truth is correspondence with outer reality or the apprehension of an object just as it is *(Yathārtha-vāda).*

The aim of life is described as the dispelling of ignorance *(Avidyā),* which obscures the true nature of the Self and God. When that is achieved, life is all bliss, although it is strictly proportionate to the intrinsic worth of each Self. The means recommended for the attainment of this state of perfect bliss are the knowledge of

God from scriptures and *Bhakti* (love of God), which in turn leads to grace *(Prasāda)*, the crowning cause of salvation.

CONCLUSION

A survey of India's philosophy, however cursory, will show that in spite of occasional lapses into inconsequential dialectic subtleties, the constant aim has been to interpret life in the concrete and to find basic means for the deliverance of man from the ills of life. This deliverance lies in the realization of the spiritual nature of man and the unity of all life. "No other path is known to the sages." This Indian emphasis on *Mokṣa* as the ultimate goal of life has often been misunderstood in the West, and Indian philosophy has consequently been accused of being other-worldly and its ethics as world-negating. Nothing could be farther from the truth, for there is no other world. There is only one world—the world of the Spirit and there is just one way, or *Marga*—the way of *Dharma.* Hindu philosophy, therefore, seeks to attain here and now the highest perfection. It emphasizes that human aspirations should be based upon the fundamental principles of *Dharma,* wherein one's good does not clash with the good of another.

The story would be incomplete without mention of Brahmo Samaj, founded by Ram Mohan Roy (1772-1833), which sought to revitalize Indian society with the age-old principle of Vedic unity; the Arya Samaj, founded by Swami Dayananda (1824-1883), re-orienting the Hindu faith on the basis of philosophical interpretation of the *Vedas;* Sri Ramakrishna Paramahamsa (1836-1886), who, speaking from the depths of realization, stressed the divine solicitude for man, and his illustrious disciple, Swami Vivekananda (1863-1902), who first transplanted Indian spirituality on Western soil; Sri Aurobindo Ghosh (1872-1950), whose poetical profundity is reminiscent of the Vedic seers and whose message of a synthetic integral *Yoga* has opened up fresh possibilities of harmonizing man's varied experience; and finally to Sri Ramana Maharishi (1879-1950), whose very existence is a demonstrable transcendence of Space and Time and a living equation of the *Ātman* with the *Brahman.* In most of these men the Vedantic temper prevailed. If the Vedantic principle of the fundamental oneness of life—as was so admirably pursued by Gandhiji in his daily life—becomes the basis of our conduct, the much coveted peace may yet be within our reach. This is, as Tagore said, the quintessence of India's spiritual philosophy, *Sāntam, Sivam, Advaitam* (Peace, Goodness, and Unity of all beings).

REFERENCES

I

Aitareya Upaniṣad
Bhagavad Gītā—Śankara Bhāsya
Brahma Sūtra Bhāsya—Śankarāchārya
Brahma Sūtra of *Bādarāyana*
Brhadāranyana Upaniṣad
Chāndogya Upaniṣad
Iśa Upaniṣad
Katha Upaniṣad
Kena Upaniṣad
Māndukyopanisad—Sānkara Bhāśya
Mīmāmsā Sūtra—Jaimini
Mundaka Upaniṣad
Nyāya Bhāśya—Vātsāyana
Nyāya Sūtra—Gautama
Praśna Upaniṣad
Rāmānuja Bhāsya on *Brahma Sūtra*
Sābara Bhāsya on *Jaimini Sūtra*
Śankhya Kārikā—Isvara Krana
Sānkhyapravacana Sūtra—Kapila
Śloka Vārttikā—Kumārila
Taittirīya Upaniṣad
Vaiśeṣika Sūtra—Kanāda
Yoga Bhāśya—Vyāsa
Yoga Sūtra—Patanjali

II

S.C. Chakravartty, *The Philosophy of the Upaniśads* (Calcutta, 1935).
Chatterji and Datta, *Introduction to Indian Philosophy* (Calcutta, 1939).
Complete Works of Swami Vivekananda, 7 vols. (Advaita Ashram, Mayavati, Himalayas, 1922).
Rhys Davids, *Letters on the Origin and Growth of Religion as Illustrated by Buddhism* (London, 1906).
J. Davies, *Hindu Philosophy* (London, 1894).
P. Deussen, *Religion and Philosophy of India* (Edinburgh, 1906).
——, *The Systems of the Vedanta.*
Aurobindo Ghosh, *Essays on the Gita* (Calcutta, 1922).
R. Guenon, *Introduction to the Study of Hindu Doctrines* (1945).
——, *Man and His Becoming according to Vedanta* (London, 1945).
S. Das Gupta, *A History of Indian Philosophy,* 3 vols. (London, 1932).
——, *Indian Idealism* (Cambridge, 1933).
M. Hiriyanna, *Essentials of Indian Philosophy* (London).
——, *Outlines of Indian Philosophy* (London, 1932).
Jagmanderlal Jaini, *Outlines of Jainism* (Cambridge, 1940).
A. A. Macdonell, *India's Past* (Oxford, 1922).
T. M. P. Mahadevan, *The Philosophy of Advaita* (London, 1938).
Swami Nikhilananda, "Hinduism," in *Religion in the Twentieth Century,* edited by Vergilius Ferm (New York, 1948).
S. Radhakrishnan, *Indian Philosophy,* 2 vols. (New York, 1927).
——, *Eastern Religions and Western Thought.*
Ramakrishna Century Committee, *The Cultural Heritage of India,* Vol. I. (Calcutta).

R. D. Ranade, *A Constructive Survey of Upanisadic Philosophy* (Poona, 1926).

Shri Krishna Saksena, "Jainism," in *Religion in the Twentieth Century*, edited by Vergilius Ferm (New York, 1948).

A. B. Shastri, *Post-Samkara Dialectics* (Calcutta, 1936).

Various Authors, *Vedanta for the Western World* (London, 1948).

Basic Tenets of Indian Philosophy

During the last century or so, an impression has been created in the minds of the educated and patriotic men both in India and in other countries that there are certain fundamental or basic tenets of Indian philosophy, or for that matter, of the Western and the Oriental philosophies as well. When one begins to enquire and examine the claim critically or a little more seriously, one fails to discover any such tenet or principle either in Eastern or Western philosophy which could properly be called as either exclusively Indian or Western, at least in the philosophical thought of these countries. I want to emphasize here the term "philosophical thought," lest it be confused with religious ideas or cultural concepts and beliefs, as is very often done in such a case. I shall a little later attempt to throw some light on the causes that might have led to this widespread belief that there are some fundamental tenets of Indian philosophy as distinguished from the fundamental tenets of Western philosophy. Before I do so, let me first examine the prevalent beliefs about the fundamental tenets of Indian philosophy about which we hear so much of from authorities on Indian philosophy.

A survey of the long history of Indian philosophical thought reveals such strong and undeniable currents and periods of all conceivable movements of thought—idealism and realism, theism and atheism, monism and pluralism, naturalism and super-naturalism—that it is almost impossible to pick up any one of these and exalt it as fundamental or basic. It is often said and popularly believed that Indian thought is dominantly idealistic, and that there was no system of materialistic thought in philosophy. First, this is not true, for we have a very powerful, vigorous, extremely daring system of materialistic philosophy associated with the name of the famous philosopher, Carvaka. Though much of this literature is not available now, enough certainly is known about it through other systems. As one of the causes of the destruction of this particular variety of literature, the hypothesis of the fanatic persecution of the unorthodox cannot be ruled out. As to the special claim of idealism in our philosophy, there is no more of it than is to be found in Western philosophy.

Closely allied to the claim of idealism or spiritualism in Indian philosophy is the not of Asceticism in Indian life. It is often proclaimed that the stress in Indian thought, in general, is on renunciation rather than on fulfillment and that a man is judged more by what he gives up rather than by what he accepts. It is not necessary to dwell upon this point, for everyone, I believe, understands the higher status given to the concepts of *tapas,* austerity, sacrifice, non-attachment and the like. To the extent this note of asceticism or renunciation stands for the inevitable truth inherent in all higher orders of life and existence, it is found to be as much a fundamental of Indian philosophy as in the basic teaching of European or Western thought. Hence, to make any philosophical capital out of asceticism in Indian thought is both to misunderstand it and to misrepresent it.

Another point often sought to be made about the peculiarity of Indian philosophy is that it is practical or that it is a way of life or realization. It is said that philosophy in India has not been pursued merely because of man's love of wisdom or the satisfaction of the demands of his intellect. It has a deeply practical motive, which is the attainment of *mokṣa,* or liberation, or the absolute cessation of the three-fold *dukkha,* or suffering.

A little reflection on Indian philosophy and its practical effect upon the lives of men in India would hardly justify the above claim. While it is true that life rather than thought and that being rather than knowing has always been regarded as more important and worthwhile in India, this has not been due to any special characteristics of the philosophical thought. This practical bias is due more to the dominance of the religious and the affective attitude than to the force of philosophical thought. The same is true of men in the West or anywhere else, where religious or secular sentiments and aspirations sway their minds. Philosophy as a dispassionate and reasoned understanding of things has nowhere made men excel in the realm of action or led them to alter the basic patterns of their lives. For that you need something much less than pure thought, or if you like, something of a different stuff. All that is practical in philosophy is necessarily suspect as pure or good philosophy. No effective action is possible nor practical result achieved without an amount of fanaticism or uncritical belief, which is a negation of the philosophical attitude and is, therefore, rightly left to the unphilosophical or the semi-philosophical drives of man's psychological makeup. This, incidentally, disposes of the charge often made against Indian philosophy that it has been responsible for India's political or material degradation. Philosophy cannot possibly play such a role, and, in fact, it has never done so, either in India or elsewhere in the world. To think thusly so, is not only to expect the impossible from philosophy but also to fundamentally misunderstand its nature and function. Neither the practical prosperity of the Western world nor its opposite in India or other underdeveloped countries of the world, is due to philosophy. The causes of the rise and fall of nations must be found in the unphilosophical part of their lives.

Another point that is very often made in connection with Indian philosophy is the emphasis on direct knowledge or the immediate intuition of the highest reality. It is said that the highest reality can be revealed to us only in an immediate intuition. In other words, while in Western philosophy stress is laid on rational knowledge, we seem to be certain that our intellect, reason, or logic is but a very imperfect instrument and is not, by nature, equal to the task of raising us to the highest attainable level. We have often heard it said that Indian philosophy is intuitive, and that in the end it leads us to mysticism. But this view, too, is not supported by one's study of comparative philosophy. There have been and still persist in the West such powerful and vigorous movements of the voluntaristic, the romantic, or the antiintellectualist systems of thought that every Indian student of comparative philosophy is almost as familiar with the foreign advocates of the intuitional way of knowing and living as he is with his own mystics in India. The same point of view is sometimes expressed a little differently by saying that Indian philosophy is more subjective than objective, or that it concerns itself more with the inner rather than with the outer reality. For a serious student of the subject, it is difficult, if not impossible, to find justification for such superficial characterization of Indian philosophy.

And now let us ask ourselves the question, what are the fundamental tenets of Indian philosophy, irrespective of consideration whether or not there is any philosophical justification for regarding them as fundamental to our philosophy? Here, I think, the very first idea that occurs to one is about the divine or the spiritual nature of the universe we live in. I think that it can perhaps be said truly that this has been one of the dominant beliefs of Indian thought, the belief that the universe is not either a haphazard creation of an unintelligent or blind power, or a methodical evolution of the inherent energy of some unconscious root matter, or *prakṛti.* In other words, Indian philosophical thought is not at all sympathetic to any naturalistic or purely materialistic interpretation of the universe in which we live. This has been one of the deeper currents of thought, the materialistic or the agnostic trends in the Indian history of thought notwithstanding.

Along with the belief in the divine or the spiritual nature of the universe in which we live, necessarily goes the belief in the ultimate moral order of the universe. We do not think that there is a lack of moral authority or law in the universe or that we could do whatever we liked without reaping the just consequences of our actions. This is what is popularly known as the inexorable law of *dharma* or *karma.* Corresponding to the law of cause and effect in the world of nature, we think and believe that in the world of human affairs and actions too, there obtains not merely a law of cause and effect but also a law of moral justice, according to which reward and punishment are ultimately meted out to us, and from which there is no escape, either in this life or in the hereafter.

And now, it will not be difficult to show that in reality it is impossible either to demonstrate the reality of these beliefs in the actual existing world, or to philosophically prove them by arguments. Neither the divine nature of the universe nor the moral nature of the world stands philosophically proved or established by any one of our philosophical systems, though they are believed in by all the orthodox systems. In fact, these happen to be the most fundamental and common beliefs of all the Hindus. It is, therefore, only proper to call these and other such beliefs the religious beliefs rather than the philosophical tenets of Indian philosophy. The same applies to our common belief regarding rebirth, transmigration of the soul, and the ultimate destiny, or the *mokṣa,* of the soul from the bondage of the material body. In our vast philosophical literature there is nowhere to be found any elaborate discussion or proof of the above. These truths (if they have the status of truths) or beliefs appear to have been taken for granted on the testimony of experts to whom they are supposed to have been revealed beyond doubt in their own direct and immediate experience. This incidentally, leads to a philosophical point of some importance. In Indian philosophical thought, testimony, or *śabda pramāṇa,* has been almost universally recognized as a valid means of proof. This has been a source of some puzzlement to some modern-minded philosophers who recognize only perception and inference as admissible means of knowledge. The question is: Should the word of a person, however reliable, be taken as a proof for purposes of knowledge? In India, we see no harm or logical error in it; and consequently, we do not hesitate to take on trust the testimony of other persons with regard to all those experiences to which, we ordinary human beings have no access either through direct perception or through reasoning. And it is hardly an exaggeration to say that almost all our so-called philosophical tenets, such as the spiritual nature of the universe, the moral law of *dharma,* the theory of rebirth *(mokṣa),* are more in the nature of beliefs taken on trust on the strength of the unimpeachability of the character of their testifiers than in the nature of proved conclusions arrived at by philosophical arguments. The same, however, is done in the Western world in the realm of higher truths of the sciences. More than nine-tenths of our knowledge of the physical, the chemical, or the medical world consist of our acceptance of the knowledge and assertions of the few experts who alone have any direct access to the validity of their truths. But, somehow, when it comes to the super-sensible, the modern Western mind reacts differently. That, however, is not to say that such religious or intuitional experiences or truths are, therefore, valid. The fact remains that the so-called fundamental tenets of Indian philosophy are mostly grounded in testimony of the seers, or the *ṛṣis,* or of the realized souls, though the average man or even a trained thinker may have no inkling of them by pure reasoning or abstract logic. The total impression left on the mind of a modern thinker about the fundamental beliefs of Indian thought is that they all lack philosophical basis and that they can hardly be called philosophical, unless the very meaning of what the Indians call "philosophical activity" is changed.

To sum up, I have tried to think of the fundamental tenets of Indian philosophy, and in so doing, I have been compelled to maintain that, strictly and philosophically speaking, no such basic tenets can be found in the long history of our philosophical thought. Even a comparison of Indian philosophical thought with Western philosophy does not reveal any such principle or truth which could be termed peculiarly Indian. Next, I examined the fundamental tenets which are commonly regarded in India as well as outside of India as the basic tenets of Indian philosophy and found no justification for calling them philosophy proper or as being founded on philosophical arguments and reasoning alone. Nevertheless, most of these truths, particularly those about the transmigration of the soul, or of the nature of *mokṣa,* and the Law of Karma remain peculiarly Indian and also fundamental to our mind. On reflection, it would, however, appear that all these fundamental tenets are more in the nature of religious beliefs and intuitions rather than the products of Indian reasoning and argument, and that is one reason why they have such a hold on our minds and consciousness. This last characteristic may make them more fundamental, but that certainly does not make them any more philosophical.

If the above reflections are sound, one may well ask how is it that belief in them as the fundamental tenets of Indian philosophy came to be so widely prevalent, both in India and abroad. Well, that is anybody's guess, but, I for one think that it is mainly due to India's contact with the West and is the first fruit of the study of India's religion and philosophy by foreigners. India has always been known to the Western world as a land of a very strange religion, and what was first studied by foreigners was its religious literature; later, these religious beliefs of the Hindus came to be regarded as their philosophical truths. In fact, there was hardly, if ever, any distinction made between India's philosophy and religion. The two were thus confused and identified. The confusion, strange to say, persists even today after more than a century's study of India's philosophy, both by Indians and by foreigners. The time, I believe, has come when students of philosophy all over the world, particularly in India, should think afresh and separate Indian philosophy from Indian religion.

Testimony in Indian Philosophy

One of the distinguishing features of Indian philosophy is that almost all the orthodox schools, in addition to other commonly accepted instruments of knowledge like perception and inference, believe in testimony*, i.e., verbal or written authority *(śabda)* as one of the valid means of knowledge *(pramāṇas)*. It is sometimes said that it is here that Indian philosophy differs most prominently from Western philosophy. Indian philosophy not only recognizes testimony among its sources of knowledge, but sometimes even accords it a higher place of importance, inasmuch as by authority alone are certain facts supposed to be known which are not capable of being revealed by other sources of knowledge. Sometimes, again, perception, inference, etc., are in the last analysis made dependent on agreement with authority. Modern Western philosophy, on the contrary, is founded upon a revolt against authority. Frequently, the history of Western philosophy impresses upon the reader the fact that, while the medieval period is characterized by belief in the authoritative character of revelation, the history of ancient and modern philosophy constitutes eras of reason and free thought. Modern philosophy is supposed to have banished the appeal to testimony, divine or secular, from rational inquiry. Authority may find recognition in religion, but has no place in philosophical and logical investigation, which recognizes only two sources of valid knowledge, i.e., the immediate source of sense perception and the mediate source of inferential reasoning.

In Western philosophy, therefore, there is supposed to be a kind of antithesis between authority and reason. One may choose to put

*The terms "testimony" and "authority" have both been used in this paper to stand for the original Sanskrit term "*śabda*," which means "the word of a reliable person." Actually, in Indian philosophy, there is no difference in the meaning of the two words, but in view of the difference in modern usage, care has been taken to use here one or the other according to what has appeared more appropriate in the given context.

one's faith in authority or elect to be rational, for belief in authority is not conceived to be rational. In Indian philosophy, however, there is no such antithesis. Belief in reason and belief in authority are both regarded as rational and valid, and hence, not only is there no antithesis between reason and authority, but there is also supposed to be none between philosophy and religion. The subject matter of both is investigated and inquired into by the same mental processes of perceptual knowledge, inferential knowledge, and knowledge derived from the statements of the experts.

Often a great distinction between Indian and Western philosophy is made on the basis of their respective differing emphases on intuition and reason. This distinction is in reality not so well founded as it is often assumed to be. In the Western philosophical tradition, there are too enduring anti-intellectual trends, and even systems of thought. In Indian philosophy, there is too much analytical, dialectical, and non-intuitional disputation to justify such a sweeping generalization. But the recognition in the Indian philosophical tradition in general of authority as a valid means of knowledge and the neglect of the same in modern Western thought is too clear and genuine to be ignored by students of comparative philosophy. While the various schools of Indian philosophy differ with regard to the exact number of the valid sources of knowledge (numbering from one to six in all, i.e., perception, inference, authority, analogy, presumption [or postulation], and non-existence), the recognition of testimony as a valid means of knowledge is one of the greatest common factors in almost all the orthodox schools of Indian philosophy. And thus, while to an outside observer Indian philosophy appears authority-ridden, so much so that reason is made to play a subservient role, Western philosophy is regarded by an Indian as having deprived itself of an important and legitimate channel of knowledge, through which alone are revealed some of our deepest truths.

The purpose of this chapter is, therefore, twofold: first, to determine the exact place of testimony in Indian logic and epistemology, and, second, to discuss in general the question as to whether or not testimony should be recognized as a valid means of knowledge.

But first of all, as a preliminary to our inquiry, we should do well to note here one or two special features of Indian philosophical thought and literature. The first, for want of a more suitable term, may be called its historical peculiarity, by which I mean that this literature as we know it today has its roots in centuries of oral tradition. All the philosophers historically known to us were preceded by a vast nameless and authorless compendium of knowledge, closely knit and guarded in cryptic lines safe and suitable for oral transmission from generation to generation. The first task, therefore, of early Indian thinkers was to interpret, explain, and coordinate this vast body of knowledge inherited and preserved by tradition rather than to function in a vacuum. This often gives to an outside observer the impression that rational thinking in India is authority-ridden or is nothing more than an interpretation of what is believed to have been already accepted as true, and that there is no original and free rational thinking beyond the spere of the already given. This is not true, however, for, as will be shown later, while Indian philosophy is also by historical circumstances interpretative, in philosophical contribution, it is no less original or daring than any other. It is not wrong, however, for intellect and reasoning to function in relation to a traditional heritage, the beginnings of which, at least in the case of India, are absolutely unknown.

Second, there is a philosophical fact of infinitely greater importance which follows from the above. Psychologically, knowing itself is defined and understood in India as necessarily involving the three steps of *śravaṇa* (hearing), *manana* (examination of what is heard), and *nididhyāsana* (realization or assimilation of what is thus reflected upon). That the first step in knowing is called *hearing* and not *perceiving* shows the verbal character of early knowledge. If an individual or an age has such a thing as tradition preceding it, one learns first by hearing. If, however, one is devoid of all tradition and has nothing to precede one's own thinking, one must look and see for oneself. But as most knowledge is first acquired by hearing from those who know more, verbal testimony is the inevitable relationship between what is learned and the source of learning. But uncritical acceptance of what is given on testimony is never expected, and that is why *manana* or a critical examination by one's own reason of what is thus learned is invariably recommended as a necessary and a prior step to the final realization of truth on the part of a seeker of true knowledge. It is, therefore, this Indian emphasis on testimony (due to the existence of traditional wisdom) as the inevitable first step of all knowledge that is also sometimes misunderstood in the West as being synonymous with truth itself in Indian philosophy, because the second and the third steps of critical reflection and final assimilation are largely lost sight of.

To begin with, therefore, we should clear up a misunderstanding which exists widely in the West with regard to the logical status of testimony in Indian philosophy. Because orthodox philosophical literature of India accepts the word of the Vedas as true and because it accepts testimony, i.e., the word of a reliable person, as an independent source of knowledge different from perception and inference. it is popularly believed that Indian philosophy accepts authority as such as true and dispenses with proof. This, however, is not the case, and we often talk at cross purposes because we do not mean the same thing by authority. Let us see first what is *not* the place of authority in Indian philosophy.

First, testimony is only a *source* of knowledge and is not, as such, to be believed or regarded as true. If it were, there would be no such thing as belief in a particular testimony (say, of the Vedas) and not in authority in general. Those who quote the words of the Vedas as authority do not accept the words of their opponents as authority. Testimony, therefore, like other valid sources of knowledge, is only the *psychological cause* of knowledge and not the *logical ground* of its truth, which is to be determined on other grounds.

Second, testimony does not annul or replace other sources of knowledge, like perception and inference. No one engaged in philosophical activity maintains that it is not necessary to perceive or reason for oneself in view of the fact that some authority is there already to give us all knowledge. This would negate the rational activity itself. Anyone acquainted with philosophical and speculative activity in India would at once see that just the reverse is the case. Actually, the entire literature of the six orthodox systems of Indian philosophy, comprising the Nyāya theory of objects of knowledge and fallacies, the Vaiśeṣika theory of atoms and numbers, the Sāṁkhya theory of the twenty-four principles, the Yoga psychology of the control of the fluctuations of mind, the Mīmāṁsā theory of the self-illuminacy and self-validity of knowledge, and the different varieties of Vedānta, is all spun out of the speculations of the minds of the different thinkers, and hardly anything more than a few suggestions, concepts, and phrases of these later developments can be made to derive from the *śrutis* (the accepted authority of the Vedas).

What, therefore, is the role of testimony in these speculations? And what constitutes the logical ground of its truth? Testimony is *one of the traditionally admitted sources of knowledge.* It is recognized that verbal or written statements of reliable persons reveal as much of the knowledge of facts to another person as his own perceptions and reasoning do. It is through testimony that a child gets his knowledge from parents or teachers, and adults know of the minds of other men and acquire knowledge of the geography and the history of the world they live in. Does Western philosophy deny that the words of another can and do furnish the dark chamber of the mind with knowledge, in addition to the two windows of sensation and reflection with which Locke furnished the mind of man? This would be contrary to our daily experience. How could Western philosophy discuss the views of other philosophers as true or false, if it did not believe them to be the views of those philosophers? Through what source, if not testimony or authority, do we believe in the records of the historians of Buddha and Christ, or even of our own contemporaries when their words come to us through other reliable persons? While we do not accept what Aristotle said as true, do we not accept what he said as what *he* said? This is itself knowledge by testimony even when we have the words of the philosophers themselves as our guide. This means that both in India and in the West we believe in testimony as a valid means of knowledge. It is impossible to deny that one believes in signs like "danger ahead," "men at work," or "sharp curve," when one is driving on the road.

When Western philosophy denies testimony, it can mean either of two things: first, that testimony as such (no matter whose) is not the same thing as truth, because it can be false, or, second, that testimony is not an independent source of knowledge but is included in perception or inference. The first is a common ground between authority and any other source of knowledge, such as perception or reasoning, for perception or reasoning also (no matter whose) cannot be regarded as necessarily true. Western philosophy does not claim to believe in all perception and inference as true. If we are to disclaim authority on this score, we might as well not believe in perception and reasoning also for the same reason. Just as all cases of perception and reasoning cannot be true, although some will be true, similarly, while all authority may not be true, some will be. But how to determine which testimony is true and which false? The answer is that the truth of testimony is proved or disproved in the same way in which the truth of any other source of knowledge is proved. Perception or inference is proved true or false by correspondence or coherence or pragmatic tests. The same is the case with the words of authority, whether of a doctor or of a religious teacher. Why not, therefore, believe in authority along with perception and inference as a valid means of knowledge when the validity of knowledge in any case depends upon other conditions? Indian philosophy does no more than recognize that some authority is true exactly as some cases of reasoning and perception are true.

The question may still be asked, "How can we know that a particular authority is right?" We must know it to be right before we can believe in it. Of course, you must know it to be right before you believe it. This is exactly what is meant by the reliability of "word." That one relies upon authority does not mean that one is called upon to believe in unverified or unverifiable authority. No one maintains that testimony or authority is above verifiability, which is again a common ground between authority and all other sources of knowledge. Authority is rejected when it no longer proves to be true. As Vasiṣṭha, one of the most revered and acknowledged authorities in Indian philosophy, says: "A reasonable statement, even of a child, should be accepted, while the unreasonable ones are to be discarded like straw, even though they are made by the Creator Himself. A devotee of Reason should value the words even of ordinary persons, provided they advance knowledge and are logical, and should throw away those of sages, if they are not such."[1] Testimony in philosophy is believed to be already tested and verified exactly as in the case of road signs. No one gets out of his car in order to see whether the bridge is really narrow after reading the sign "narrow bridge ahead." You first believe in your road signs (or in the words of the doctor) and that provides an opportunity for the test or verification of the truth or the falsity of the testimony. Verifiability itself would not be possible if one did not admit these signs and words as valid *sources* of knowledge to begin with. While verifiability tests the truth or falsity of knowledge, it does not produce it. What is contended here is that knowledge should first be admitted for the time being as true on testimony before you can verify and accept or reject it as true or false. The validity of belief in authority lies solely and exclusively in its reliability. And it is this reliability of the word of another that is recognized as an independent valid source of knowledge in Indian philosophy. This reliability is based entirely upon verifiability. No orthodox Indian system of philosophy says that the words of the Vedas may be false and yet you should believe in them. The orthodox systems only say that they have been established as true and are hence reliable. If you can prove that they are false, they will not be reliable and hence will not constitute authority. But this will be a disbelief only in the Vedas, i.e., the authoritativeness of a particular testimony, but not disbelief in authority itself as a valid means of knowledge.

Now, what is such a valid means of knowledge that finds such an important place in philosophical discussions in orthodox schools of Indian philosophy? Questions relating to the origin and the validity of knowledge are the core of philosophical discussion, and, ever since the time of Locke, epistemology has been a prolegomena to any serious metaphysics in the West. Indian philosophy bestowed serious attention upon the question of the origin and validity of knowledge much earlier than did philosophy in the West. Both in India and in the West, a distinction has always been drawn between opinion and knowledge, between rumor, hearsay, or the personal whims of an individual and what is regarded as psychologically valid sources of knowledge. Obviously every source of knowledge cannot be recognized as acceptable. The question therefore is asked as to what and how many are those independent sources through which alone we rightly acquire our knowledge of fact. *This question of the valid sources of knowledge is not to be confused with the related question of the truth of the knowledge thus acquired.* The question "How do we know what we know?" and the question "How do we know that what we know is true?" are two entirely different questions, and must be constantly kept apart if the issue of authority as a valid means of knowledge is to be clearly apprehended.

In Western philosophy, sense perception and inference have been regarded as the commonly accepted instruments of knowledge since the beginning of the Renaissance, and Western philosophers have almost unanimously accepted the exhaustiveness of these two sources and have seldom questioned their adequacy. Indian philosophers, on the other hand, recognize that our entire body of knowledge at no period of time could be completely accounted for or explained by sense perception and inference alone. We always know much more than can be accounted for by our own perception or inference. In fact, it is incontestable that at any given time verbal testimony accounts for nine-tenths of our stock of knowledge. The question, therefore, is, "Should authority be recognized as an independent and valid means of knowledge?" To answer this question, we must know, first of all, what authority is and what exactly is meant by testimony? Gautama, as one of the greatest expounders of authority, defines authority or "word" in his *Nyāya-sūtra*—the classical text of the traditional "Logical school" of Indian philosophy—as "the assertion of a reliable person,"[2] and this definition stands generally accepted and adopted by all other Indian systems. A reliable person is further defined in the *Nyāya-bhāṣya* on the same *sūtra* as one "who possesses the direct and right knowledge of things, who is moved by a desire to make known [to others] the thing as he knows it, and who is fully capable of speaking of it."[3] It is interesting to note here that the Nyāya system does not mean by authority divine revelation or scriptural testimony only, but, contrary to the belief of other schools, adds that such a reliable person may be a sage, any ordinary person, or, in fact, anyone. It is further held that it is not at all necessary that such a person should be completely free from moral defects. What is needed is that he should have no motive to give incorrect information—a fact which accords completely with our modern attitude toward authority or the testimony of experts. Testimony is further subdivided into two kinds: *viz.*, testimony based upon things perceived, and testimony based upon things heard and inferred though not seen. A man may, for instance, speak of what he has himself seen, or he may speak of what he has heard or inferred. Either of these could be an equally valid source of knowledge to others.

Now, with regard to authority as a valid source of knowledge, two questions can be raised immediately. First, "Should authority be accepted at all as a valid source of knowledge?" and, second, "If accepted, what should be its place in relation to other means of knowledge?" Is it just like any other source of information giving valid knowledge, or does it enjoy a greater authoritativeness and a place of privilege over perception, inference, and the rest? As to the latter, it is maintained that there is no such thing as a higher and lower validity of knowledge, for the idea of quantity is not admissible in the concept of validity as such. What distinguishes the different means of valid knowledge such as perception, inference, and authority from one another is not their higher or lower validity but the nature and kind of facts and objects which they reveal. Perceptual knowledge, e.g., reveals the externally and sensuously perceptible world; inference employs a non-sensuous process and applies it to the abstract and the remote, and authority helps us to cognize what cannot be known by either of the other sources of knowledge. Any one of these could be equally valid or invalid in its own sphere, and there is no point in saying that one is more valid than the other. That testimony is supposed to reveal knowledge of facts like *dharma, mokṣa,* etc., which are in themselves considered to be of more importance to man than knowledge of facts about the sensible world, or that the scriptures are supposed to contain knowledge which is considered to have been acquired by minds higher than our own, is, however, quite another matter. Here, one may ask, is it not a fact that in Indian philosophy a man's reasoning and conclusions are *ipso facto* invalidated if they are not in agreement with the authority of the Veda and the Upaniṣads—called *śruti?* Does this not undermine the independent validity of other sources of knowledge like inference, etc., and lead to their subordination to authority? No. As Śaṅkara himself says, "Scriptures cannot be acknowledged to refute that which is settled by other means of right knowledge."[4] Besides, the agreement sought here is not between inference and authority, i.e., between one means of knowledge and another, but between the reasoning of a higher and a lower mind. Even at the level of perception or reasoning, we always measure and seek agreement between our reasoning and that of those better trained and skilled than ourselves. We always compare lower reasoning with higher reasoning. We do not seek correspondence between our inferences and those of children, imbeciles, and idiots. Among reasonable people also, what is reasonable to one man is not so to another, and we seek to tally our rational conclusion with those recognized to be the most perfect in the field. There is thus no subordination of reason to authority—but only of lower reason to higher reason, and it is difficult to see how one can object to this distinction and practice in general, even though we may not agree as to the particular person or persons who possess a more rational or perfect mind. Those in India, therefore, who deny the authority of the Vedas refuse to believe them as the knowledge of minds higher than their own. In fact, the Cārvākas called the Vedas the prattlings of insane minds. That, however, is not the same as disbelief in the word of a reliable person.

As to the recognition of testimony as a means of valid knowledge, no question has even seemed to have arisen in India. That we actually know and learn by testimony is a matter of indubitable fact, and thus it is as valid as any other source, such as perception. The only objection raised in India against testimony has been on the score of its independence, i.e., that knowledge by testimony is not an independent source of knowledge, but is a variety of perception or inference. There is no need, therefore, for the recognition of authority as a separate source of knowledge, and this is the second reason why Western philosophy may also deny authority. This argument is discussed at length,[5] and it is conclusively established that knowledge by verbal or written testimony cannot be included in the category of sensation and ideation, for it does not possess the differentia of perception or inference. Perception requires that the senses be in contact with an external object, and this is not so in the case of testimony, for, when a word is apprehended, it is the inner meaning and not the outer sound which is the object of knowledge. Similarly, it is contended that, for lack of a middle term and "universal concomitance," testimony cannot be classed as inference. Also, there is no such positive thing present in inference as the word of a reliable person which is the chief distinguishing mark of authority. That is why this *pramāṇa* is called *śabda*, or "word," to indicate clearly its differentia. Here, knowledge is acquired not through any universal connection but solely because of the reliability of the word of a certain person. Praśastapāda, one of the Vaiśeṣika objectors to testimony, in his *bhāṣya* on the *Vaiśeṣika-sūtra*, says, "Words and the rest are also included in inference because they have the same principle," i.e., testimony also functions in the same way as inference. When the Vaiśeṣika system maintains that the knowledge derived from "word" is inferential, what is meant is that words also give knowledge by force of a universal connection just as smoke gives rise to the knowledge of fire.[6] Similarly, the Buddhist logician Diṅnāga in his *Pramāṇa-samuccaya* asks, "What is the significance of the credible word? Does it mean that the person who spoke the word is credible or that the fact he averred is credible?"[7] In either case, the means of knowledge is either inference or perception. We have learned from experience that as a general rule the statements of reliable persons are true, and we apply this experience to the case of the particular statement. To this the Nyāya reply is that the opponent has not understood the meaning of cognition by verbal indication, and that, as explained above, he means by *pramāṇa* quite another thing. When we consider that the Naiyāyika and the Bauddha both hold that the means of knowledge do not carry their own validity with them but it must be separately established from some other source, it is difficult to understand how the Bauddhas can refuse to admit "word" as a separate *pramāṇa*. This confusion is due to the fact that, while the Nyāya is speaking of "word" as a psychological cause of knowledge, the Bauddha is speaking of knowledge as true or false. "Word" *(śabda)* is thus to be regarded as quite an independent source of knowledge, which is not covered under any one of the other sources of knowledge.

The second objection to authority points out the fact that testimony is often false and contradictory. It therefore cannot be accepted as valid. This argument of the opponents of authority is regarded as based on pure prejudice, for it is obvious that this defect is no peculiarity of authority alone, but is common to perception, inference, and any other source of knowledge which may be regarded as valid. Our perceptions, inferences, and analogies can all be wrong and contradictory and do often turn out to be so when they stand in need of correction, but no one refuses to recognize them on that account as valid means of knowledge. Neither perception, nor inference, nor any other source of knowledge is valid as such, for their validity is to be established independently of their origin, unless, of course, like the *Mīmāṁsakas,* we hold that all cognitions produced from whatever source are valid as such. We are again confusing sources of knowledge and criteria of their truth or falsity. What is contended is nót that the word of a reliable person is true as such, but that we rightly regard it as true until the contrary is established quite in the same manner as we regard our perceptions. Moreover, this objection of the opponent is not against all testimony, but only against a particular testimony, a fact to which all the orthodox Indian philosophers would readily agree. The conclusion is unavoidable, therefore, that testimony is as much a valid source of knowledge as perception or inference. There is thus no reason for not including authority among the valid sources of knowledge.

Granting testimony as an independent source of knowledge, the question may now be asked as to wherein the validity of testimony actually lies. The answer is that it lies in the trustworthiness of the speaker and that this trustworthiness is always as verifiable as that of any other means of knowledge, like signs on the road or the words of a doctor. The *Nyāya-sūtra* continues: "The Trustworthiness of the Word (of the Veda) is based upon the trustworthiness of the reliable (veracious) expositor, just like the trustworthiness of Incantations and of Medical Scriptures."[8] The *Bhāṣya* again raises the question "In what does the trustworthiness of the Medical Scriptures consist?" and the answer given is that it consists in verification. "It consists in the fact that, when the Medical Scriptures declare that 'by doing this and this one obtains what he desires, and by avoiding this and this he escapes from what is undesirable'—and a person acts accordingly,—*the result turns out to be exactly as asserted;* and this shows that the said Scriptures are *true,* not *wrong* in what they assert."[9] What is important for us, however, is to note that it is on the basis of verifiability alone that the Vedas are believed to be reliable and hence authoritative by the orthodox systems. It is quite another matter, if an opponent regards the same as unreliable as a result of unverifiability, for the ground of belief or disbelief in both cases would be the same.

It is necessary to close the discussion with a final reiteration. In Indian philosophical discussion, the term *pramāṇa* is used in the sense of a psychological cause of knowledge, but it is a logical concept also inasmuch as it limits the validity of such causes to only a few of the many possible causes of knowledge; for instance, rumor or hearsay is not regarded as a valid source of knowledge. Translated into English, *pramāṇa* is rendered as "valid means of knowledge," the term *valid* applying to the *means* and not to the *knowledge*. The *pramāṇas* are not the means of *valid knowledge*, but only *valid means* of knowledge, the validity of which is always to be determined by other means. Thus, when the orthodox Indian systems believe in authority as a valid means of knowledge, they do not imply that all testimony is valid, but only that authority is one of the valid means of knowing. When a Westerner opposes authority, he imposes upon authority a validity which is not intended in the Indian recognition of authority as a *pramāṇa*, or he is imposing extra conditions upon authority's being accepted as valid from which he frees perception and inference. Not to include testimony in the sense of the word of a reliable person in one's list of valid sources of knowledge is to reject *prima facie* a vast body of knowledge from the field of philosophical inquiry, and that is hardly justifiable. For such facts as are necessarily revealed by authority alone cannot openly and without prejudice be investigated unless we accept them as the valid data of our knowledge. To refuse to admit testimony as a means of knowledge because not all testimony is true is to throw away the baby with the bath. It is the sheer prejudice of centuries that has unreasonably made Western philosophy blindly ignore the value of knowledge by testimony in philosophy, while retaining it in all other fields. To end with another quotation from the *Bhāṣya:* "In ordinary worldly matters also, a large amount of business is carried on on the basis of the assertions of veracious persons; and here also the trustworthiness of the ordinary veracious expositor is based upon the same three conditions—he has full knowledge of what he is saying, he has sympathy for others (who listen to him), and he has the desire to expound things as they really exist;—and on the basis of these the assertion of the veracious expositor is regarded as trustworthy."[10]

NOTES

1. *Yoga Vasiṣṭha*, II. 18. 2,3. Quoted by B.L. Atreya, *The Philosophy of the Yoga-Vasiṣṭha* (Adyar, Madras: The Theosophical Publishing House, 1936), p. 581.
2. Ganganatha Jha, *Gautama's Nyāyasūtras* (Poona: Oriental Book Agency, 1939), p. 29; I. i. 7.
3. *Ibid.*, p. 30; *Nyāya-bhāṣya*, I. i. 7.
4. F. Max Müller, trans., *Vedānta-sūtras with Śaṅkara's Commentary*, Sacred Books of the East, Vol. XXXIV Part I (Oxford: Clarendon Press, 1890), p. 318; II. i. 13. Or, "Śruti, if in conflict with other means of right knowledge, has to be bent so as to accord with the latter"

(*Ibid.*, p. 229); or again, "Moreover, the scriptural passage, 'He is to be heard, to be thought,' enjoins thought in addition to hearing, and thereby shows that Reasoning also is to be resorted to with regard to Brahman" (*Ibid.*, p. 300).

5. Jha, *op. cit.*, pp. 177-184; *Nyāya-sūtra,* II. i. 50-57.
6. B. Faddegon, *The Vaiçeṣika-system* (Amsterdam: Johannes Muller, 1918), pp. 465-474.
7. S.C. Vidyabhusana, *A History of Indian Logic* (Calcutta: Calcutta University, 1921), p. 288.
8. Jha, *op. cit.*, p. 191; *Nyāya-sūtra,* II. i. 69.
9. *Ibid.*, p. 192; *Nyāya-bhāṣya,* II. i. 69. Italics mine.
10. *Ibid.*, p. 193; *Nyāya-bhāṣya,* II. i. 69.

Hinduism

SOME SPECIAL CHARACTERISTICS

Hinduism stands for the religious ideas and practices of the Hindus in India, but the term "Hindu" itself is given by foreigners to the inhabitants of India. The religion of the Hindus in their own language is called *Sanātan Dharma,* meaning literally the "eternal religion." This religion is different from the other great religions of the world because it was not founded by any single prophet or son of God. It is the name for the dominant religious and moral thoughts of all the persons who have lived in India from almost prehistoric times to the present. These thoughts are preserved in what are called the authoritative texts, *Śruti,* or whatever has been "heard" from the elders. Technically, these texts are called the Vedas, the Brāhamaṇas, and the Āranyakas. More or less the same ideas are popularly expressed in the epics of the *Rāmāyana* and the *Mahābhārata,* the *Bhagavad-Gītā,* the semi-historical books of tales and legends of the ancient times, called the Purāṇas, which are called the *Smṛtis,* or "remembered" ones. Hinduism is claimed by its adherents to be a universal religion for man in general, for all times, and not for the Hindus alone.

Another feature of Hinduism is that, in spite of its being claimed as an eternal and an ever-present religion, it has no desire to propagate its religion to the followers of other religions. It is thus one of the most non-missionary and non-proselytizing religions in the world, though, by the late nineteenth and early twentieth centuries, attempts were made by the Ārya Samāja, a reformist sect of the Sanātan Dharma, to take the non-Hindus converted to Christianity and Islam back into the fold of Hinduism. But that attempt has been given up. Anyone can become a Hindu or may call himself a Hindu without any Hindu wanting him to become a Hindu. Hinduism believes that since all great religions recommend the same moral principles of daily living, and since all religions have their own ideas of a god as the ruler of the universe to whom they can psychologically adapt by prayer and worship, what is important is that a non-Hindu be a better follower of his own religion than that he change his religion to that of another place or time, since these historical accidents do not make a religion true or false. The idea in this kind of catholicity and essential identity of all religions is not to demonstrate that the religions of the world do not differ in numerous ways, but only that these differences in themselves are not so important as is their fundamental identity which, if truly followed, makes a man lead a noble life.

Hinduism gives freedom to its adherents in the matter of prayer and worship and in the concept of gods and goddesses in their different aspects. To a Westerner it may be surprising to note that Hinduism has no church and has no ecclesiastical organization. It has no structural administrative unity for the purpose of guiding the religious life of its adherents. Hinduism is not an organized machinery of religiosity which is to take care of the religious life of its followers or spread the religion to outsiders. The Hindu religious precepts are all deeply rooted in the minds and hearts of millions of men and women who follow its pious doctrines, pray, and build temples freely whenever and wherever they like, in any structure and form. They also install their own deities, pray and worship in their own way, and derive their own solace and comfort. This variety and freedom in Hinduism often bewilders foreigners who are unable to calculate the actual number of deities or gods or goddesses in Hinduism. Outsiders have called Hinduism by many names: pantheism, polytheism, and other types of theisms. This, however, does not bother the Hindus who see a subjective and psychologically identical attitude working in religious minds towards their different gods or goddesses. Also, they all have the same moral code for their daily practices. These differences therefore are regarded as external and unimportant and are freely permitted. Actually, the genius of the Hindus through the centuries has been to see and assert the essential unity in the midst of the manifold and necessary diversities and to let the diversities remain where they do not damage the existence and the practical value of the essential unity. The subjective unification of mind and heart is regarded as more important than the objective diversification of practice, which must be the case with human beings in different conditions—accidents of time, place, history, and education. The Hindus have always carried this craze for oneness or unity in the midst of diversity into fields other than religion.

FUNDAMENTAL BELIEFS

GOD

What are the fundamental religious beliefs of the Hindus? The first religious belief of the Hindus is in the reality of the existence of God, as the one, unborn, eternal and universal spirit, immanent and transcendent in the universe as its Supreme Being. He is the inward ruler of the universe, dwelling in all things and in the heart of man. He is the guarantee and the justification of the reality of the moral values in the universe. We need not go into the different philosophical theories of the Hindus about the nature of God and His relation to the universe and man. Suffice it to say that these philosophical theories, being free from emotional attachments, do not usually affect man's relationship to his God. The Hindus therefore agree in the conception of God in His two different aspects called the *Nirguna* ("attributeless God") and the *Saguna* ("God with attributes"). In his religious life, a Hindu worships God in the "full-of-attributes form" which includes an infinity of His attributes of perfect knowledge, power, and love. It is this God with infinite attributes upon whom a Hindu is expected to meditate and to incorporate the effects of his devotion and meditation toward the development of his spiritual life. Also with *Saguna*, or the full-of-attributes form of God, it is to be remembered that the one Perfect and the Universal Spirit is not logically expected to possess all these infinite and perfect attributes which cannot be apprehended through the limited and finite intellect of man. Nor can the mind of man form a mental picture of such a Reality. Man is, therefore, allowed to have any symbol of God for his worship. This symbol can be any form or shape—a stone, a tree, a mythological figure—representing any god or goddess which, in the mind of the devotee, is a symbol of his own God. God is indescribable and incomprehensible. This is His *Nirguna Rūpa*, or attributeless form. Though simple, this principle is usually not understood in its proper perspective by an outsider who sees hundreds of temples in India adorned with different gods and goddesses. When India first came into contact with the Western world, the foreigners called Hinduism an idolatrous religion and the Hindus idol worshippers. Actually, this is far from being true, for Hindus are the only people who stress and emphasize the fact that there can be no likeness, no picture, or no image of God, but man has to have a symbol to stand for his God.

Usually God is worshipped in His three distinct functions: the creator, or Bhramā; the sustainer, or Vishnu; and the destroyer, or Śiva. The Hindu, while he creates these symbols or images of his God in order to have a concentrated idea of any one of His attributes or name or form *(Nāma,* or *Rūpa)* to assist him in his psychological development toward divine realization, is not establishing any idol of the Supreme Being called God, or Īshvara.

The Hindus also believe that *Nirguna,* or the attributeless Divine Being takes a human form from time to time. When the laws of God are forsaken or downtrodden by human beings, He comes to the earth, lives, moves and has His being among men in this empirical and historical world. By His life on this earth He reveals the ways of God to man. This is technically called the doctrine of the *Divine Avatāra,* or the descent of the Divine in human form. To the present time in the history of Hinduism, ten such *Avatāras* have been recognized. The names of Rama, Krishna, and Buddha are among the most famous. According to traditional belief, the last *Avatāra* is still to come before this present cycle of creation is to be dissolved. The idea of this doctrine is that man by himself cannot be expected to rise to the Divine level, unless he is helped by the Divine in the ascent from the human to the Divine. All religions, in some form or other, believe in the necessity of God's *Avatāra,* or His incarnation in a concrete historical manifestation. Hinduism does not say that any particular prophet is the only son of God; rather, it believes that there can be many sons of God at various times.

THE LAW OF DHARMA

The next belief of the Hindus concerns the moral nature and structure of the universe. The universe is moral because there is a God in it, or one might say that the universe itself is divine. The world of inorganic and organic nature is not just an evolution of an unconscious material power or force creating and expressing itself in a world of greater complexity and heterogeneity by its own unconscious dialectic. It is a world of divine and spiritual immanence with the fullest reality of moral values and forces flowing from *Śakti,* or the power of God. Corresponding to the laws of nature, there are ethical laws in cosmos pertaining to moral living called the Laws of *Ṛta,* or the *Dharma.* The immanence of God is a guarantee for it. What is meant in Hinduism by moral structure of the universe is that no purely naturalistic or merely humanistic interpretation of the universe is going to justify the ultimate reality of our moral values. Without this ultimate justification the world of human beings with all its culture and civilization and its rich complexity and novelty of the numerous mental and moral evolutes in it will hardly be different in essence from the world of either inorganic matter or organic life.

THE LAW OF KARMA

This introduces us to the next Hindu belief, the Law of Karma, or action, which is one of the most well known but least understood by Westerners. The Law of Karma is the renaming of the universally accepted law of causation as applied in the rational and the ethical realms of a man's life. It says that it is a law of the universe that a good action must bear a good result and that a bad action must end in a bad result. It does not only say that it should be so but also that the universe is so constituted that is is so. We cannot pass from an "ought" to a necessary "is." In fact, we pass from an "is" to an "ought," that is, from reality to ideality, and not from our ideality to reality.* Without a firm belief in the Law of Karma, in the sense of being morally responsible for our actions, there is no reason why a sinful man should be different from a sage. This Law of Karma has nothing to do with any doctrine of predestination of a man's actions, or with anything which will make a man a fatalist, or an escapist. Inasmuch as a man is determined by what he has already done in the past and is free to determine what he would like to do in the future, he is both determined and free. In either case he must reap the moral fruits of his deeds. The Law of Karma is just a prerequisite and a presupposition of any moral theory of human conduct. In modern Western ideas also, individuals are supposed to be personally responsible for what they do. Hinduism takes this responsibility to be more real than based only on the force of human society or government or one's own moral conscience. The Hindus have made their ethical laws and values so real that they would obtain in the world even without any human beings in it, if such were the case. The Hindus do not understand how any ethical theory can justify morality or ethics without the existence of an inexorable moral law like other laws of nature in the universe, so that no human being can escape the fruits of his good or bad deeds, even though there be no human agency in the world to dispense the moral rewards and punishments. We

* Suppose we say that we should not kill another living man or that we should love all living beings. It does not mean that our ideal of non-killing or loving is real in the sense that it actually operates in the universe, but rather, that we would like it to operate and to come into being. The Law of Karma goes much beyond this. It says that, though we do not perceive it, all our moral values we believe in are actually and really existent in the universe as its ethical Law of Dharma which the Law of Karma must follow.

receive the morally appropriate rewards and punishments for our actions even as we receive the physical rewards for such actions as touching a fire or putting our hands into freezing water. This is what is meant by the Law of Karma. Firm belief in the Law of Karma has made the Hindus more Dharma-minded and God-fearing than other races in the world.

MAN, IMMORTALITY, AND REINCARNATION

From the Supreme Being, or God, and the objective and the eternal reality of the Dharma, or the moral nature of the universe, we move on to man. Like all other theistic religions, Hinduism believes man to be finite, an unborn and undying spirit, completely different from the complex of his body and mind. But the Hindus have gone theoretically a little deeper into the implications of a man's immortality with reference to its psychological and moral nature of the self. This has led them to believe not only in a single life on this earth but in an unending series of continued lives called the theory of *Āvāgaman,* or reincarnation, literally "coming and going." According to this theory, the immortal spirit in man reincarnates itself after each death, in a better or a worse form of life, according to the demands of man's psychological ambitions and the necessity of the ethical rewards and punishments of his actions. In other religions of the world, this need for ethical justice is justified by the theory of a day of final judgment after a single life, which, though considered by the Hindus as purely a matter of simple faith, is perhaps equally successful for the justification of the moral needs of life. It is not contended that the Hindu theory of reincarnation is as certain as any other empirical fact, but, theoretically, it seems more consistent with the demands of reason and empirical continuity inasmuch as something more is considered to be necessary for moral justice than a mere belief that ultimately all psychological and ethical differences in a man's life are somehow to be computed before the final dissolution of the universe. This does not, to the Hindu, explain the original differences of birth, heredity, and the circumstances of a man's life which are the root of all the injustice to him. The two Hindu theories of reincarnation and the Law of Karma are held to be more consistent with the causal needs of having a proper beginning and ending to a single life of unaccountable differences of heredity and destiny between men. Since nothing can come out of nothing, and since something existing cannot just pass out of existence, man has to be somewhere before he is born and after he is dead without loss of his identity. Life passes from existence to existence until all the psychological drives of man, his *Karmas*, are completely fulfilled or dried out of him. When he has attained his liberation from the bodily and earthly existence, the final goal of human life or freedom, or *Moksa*, from the bondage of continually living and dying is achieved.

MOKSA, OR ABSOLUTE FREEDOM, AND ETHICAL LIFE

The most important fundamental belief of the Hindus is that of *Moksa*, or the ultimate freedom or the liberation of man. This belief is similar to those of other great religions of the world which believe that man's actual life on this earth is not the best, the highest, or the most perfect form of human life of which he is capable. Man's life on earth is an embodied, earthly life where he is bound by the chains of pleasure and pain, joy and sorrow, the continuous changes of health, disease, old age, and death, and with the changes in his love and hate, etc. All these cause suffering and pain. The supreme purpose or the final goal of life, therefore, is to achieve an absolute freedom from the imperfections of this kind of existence or from sufferings of all kinds. This can be attained only when man has realized completely his spiritual and divine nature and has freed himself from the bonds of matter and earthly life, though he may continue to live on this earth after the attainment of his *Moksa*. A life of God-realization, of living, moving, and having his being in God is a man's salvation. Hinduism believes that all men finally attain godhood sooner or later because man is a part of God. No one, however ignorant and sinful, is therefore to be condemned forever from attaining to His truly divine nature. Sin, on the part of man, is only delaying the attainment of his destined goal. *Moksa* is a name for a divine, godly or a purely spiritual life. While there are some variations to the theoretical meaning of the concept of *Moksa*, and many philosophical questions are asked and answered about it (like that of the definite and precise relationship between the finite self of man and the infinite self of God) and while there are intellectually different answers given the same question, there is agreement upon the nature of the Divine life, of the spiritual and mystical realization of it, and of its being completely different from the lower and unspiritual life without God. In fact, of all the religions in the world, Hinduism has done the most in training men to lead a saintly and godly life, and there have been more saints and good men in India than anywhere else. Good men who have devoted their lives solely to the seeking and the perfection of their spiritual life by experiments upon themselves are called Yoga and Tantra, even as man today is exclusively devoting himself to turning into a robot. No people on earth have devoted themselves to so much deliberation on differences between dead matter and animal life and rational man, between this life here and now and a life hereafter, between the material and the spiritual, and between the empirical and the transcendental as have the Hindus. Also, no people have been so influenced by their own findings in the spiritual and the religious realms of men's emotions and actions. The most valuable aspect of the early Indian heritage is the experiences in the realms of the Yoga and Vedānta. Once upon a time India was supposed to be a land of holy men, of men good in themselves as an end. The Hindus have not been able to think of a good man without God, which is still regarded as heterodoxy. The greatest stress in Hinduism has been on living a good and a moral life here in this world so that one may bring nearer the day of his final salvation. This good life consists mainly of the conquest of certain primary and basically undesirable emotions and sentiments, like those of fear, hate, greed, and excessive attachment in daily life. The greatest *Dharma* of a man has been the practice of the law of non-hurting, or *Ahimsā,* or as it is called in Sanskrit *Ahimsā paramo dharmah.* It may be remarked here that only the Hindus have made no distinction in the practice and the concept of love between the higher life of man and the lower life of animals. That is the reason Hindus have been vegetarians and non-meat-eating peoples; they do not want to destroy another life for their own sensual enjoyment of food eating. Hinduism, as said earlier, is the common name for the prevalent moral and religious ideas and beliefs of the peoples of India, from the near prehistoric, Aryan, Brahmanic, and to the later times. We do not contend that these ideas have not changed from time to time. In fact, some of these ideas are the synthesis or catholic blend of India's contacts with the ideas and cultures of many different races and the early peoples who came from the northwest borders, but the basic beliefs have remained the same in content. In spite of India's fullest emphasis on the varied and positive enjoyments of her secular and worldly life, and with all the wealth of material goods with her at a time when no country in the world was so rich and prosperous, the Hindus have always laid much greater stress on transcending the lower secular life to a more powerful and higher ethical and spiritual life. This is evidenced by the higher values which are unfailingly given to the conquest of one's worldly desires for power over women and wealth. A craving for sex and money as ends in themselves, in

Hinduism and in most religions of the world, is the greatest bane and hurdle to the attainment of the spiritual life. The good life in Hinduism, in fact, has been conceived of as the conquest of the four deadly sins: *Kāma,* or sexual propensities; *Krodha,* or anger and hatred; *Lobha,* or the greed for earthly goods; and *Moha,* or attachment to selfish personal ties. More stress in Hindu ethics is laid on the goodness of thoughts and feelings than on mere conformity in action to the external needs of a right life. Right thinking and feeling and right speech are considered basic to right actions. The inner psychological life is more important than the outward life.

The Three Mārgas

The Hindu mind, consistent with its disposition of the acceptance of individual freedom and differences of attitude and talent between men has long recognized the validity of different *Mārgas,* or paths, as means to the attainment of the same end and the supreme goal of life. It is not considered necessary for all men to be harnessed to the same discipline for the attainment of *Moksa.* Different persons, according to their special and individual aptitudes, interests, and qualifications of their minds, can attain the same goal provided that with single-minded devotion they pursue the ideal according to their own disposition and testament. Being keenly aware of the psychological differences between men, the Hindus had recognized long before the advent of modern psychology that the mind of man was a three-aspect mind, expressing itself through knowing, feeling, and willing, or popularly cognition, affection, and conation. Some persons are born with a natural gift and predeliction for abstract thinking and reasoning, others are born with a finer sensitiveness to feelings, while others are endowed with a greater will to do things and to accomplish deeds in the outside world. The Hindus, accepting all the three as equally valid ways of fulfillment, therefore laid down the three famous paths or ways to *Moksa,* namely, that of *Jñāna,* or knowledge, that of *Bhakti,* or devotion, and that of *Karma,* or action. Since *Yoga* means both application or discipline and also union, these *Mārgas* are fittingly called the *Jñāna yoga,* the *Bhakti yoga,* and the *Karma yoga.* The idea is that there is no one, single path to the Divine Union or the attainment of the highest for man, for the same goal can be reached by different persons starting from different places and following different ways. All roads lead to the same ultimate goal. It is sometimes felt by certain persons that, though it is true a man can reach the same place by different routes, it does not follow that all routes are equally good or authentic. Since all men are not at the same place, it follows that there is no single route for all men. There must be one shortest route and, therefore, the authentic one. There is a shortest route for everyone, but it is not the same route for all. Men are not equally endowed by nature in their gifts of reason, feeling, and capacity to act, and, therefore, it is not necessary to force men to follow any single path of knowledge, emotion, or action. Attainment of the ultimate goal of life is like a process of education. There is a shortest and an authentic way to be educated, but it is not the same in content for everyone. All men need not be required to excel in the same sphere. Rather, as in education, we encourage a person to follow his or her natural inclinations and talents which he or she happens to be endowed with, the same is true with regard to our religious training also. Does it mean, therefore, that all the ways that a man can take are the paths toward God-realization? The answer is both yes and no. It is "yes" because all men are bound to fulfill their ultimate destiny sooner or later, and "no" because for each one, a particular path will be shorter than another. While the ethical requirements will be the same and identical for all of us, within this moral objectivity and oneness, all men can take to their own and individual paths of finding their fulfillment through any of the three paths: knowledge, devotion, or action. Hinduism has therefore equally recognized the greatness of not only those men who like Gandhi have been great in the world of action, but also those who like Paramhansa Ramakrishna have spent their lives in pure devotion to God, or those who like Śankara or Aurobindo Ghose have been great philosophers. Though there have been and still are great debates and disputes among philosophers about the claims of each of these *Mārgas* for relative supremacy, the prophets of all the three paths have flourished in India with equal claims on the minds of the present-day Hindus, showing once again the great genius of the people in asserting their faith in the doctrine of an essential unity in the midst of diversity and differences.

The Four Āśramas

No account of Hinduism as a religious force and as a philosophy can perhaps be considered as complete without an account of the rationale of not only the four *Puruśārthas,* or the goals of life *(Dharma, Artha, Kāma,* and *Moksa),* but also of the four *Āśramas,* or the stages of an individual's life, and the fourfold *Varna* classification of human society, called the *Varna-āśramas.* We are not concerned here with these concepts losing their original rationale and spirit and having rusted and petrified into the evils of the caste system and the tolerance of beggary in Indian society. These evils are being well looked after and are being abolished by the present government and the people. But these two doctrines form an integral part of that complex which is known as Hinduism and which, in intention, is expected to be an eternal ideal for all societies and individuals.

Life in modern times is lived mainly through two stages: first is the stage of studentship, training, and education; second is the stage of the rest of our lives in this world, that of a householder and a family man. If men live long enough, they sometimes lead what is called a retired life. This means that they are not actively engaged in any special work or job but are simply living a quiet and inactive life, occupying their time with such pursuits as their interests dictate. This retired life is not very different in quality from the previous life of activity excepting that one does not have any regular job. But persons who make their living independently may not slacken their activity or retire from their life-pursuits until the hour of their death. Against this modern way of life the Hindus, having kept before them, a higher and a more difficult goal of life, namely *Moksa* which is dependent on a more exacting ethical perfection of human nature, organized their lives to be lived ideally in four stages instead of the present two. The first and the second stages, the *Brahmacarya,* or the life of celibacy, and the *Grhastha,* or the householder, are common with those of today. Two more have been added, *Vanāprastha,* or retirement, and *Sanyāsa,* or the life of a free and unattached mendicant. Each stage is roughly divided into periods of twenty-five years; the average span of human life is considered to be about a hundred years. Having acquired education, having married, having brought up children, and having seen them married and settled them, by about age fifty, a man is supposed to have fulfilled all his normal family and social obligations. Not only is he supposed to have fulfilled his obligations and deem himself to be a freer man, he is supposed also to have fulfilled himself with regard to his desires for wealth, women, and such sensuous and worldly enjoyments. He is supposed to have acquired a "sense of enoughness" about worldly means to certain necessary ends, and should now give up this worldly and sensuous life, and retire for another twenty or twenty-five years to a place of relative quietness and calm perfecting his nature psychologically and morally. He should be able to live the last twenty-five years of his life as a *Sanyāsin.* Whenever a man feels that he has no ties of personal emotions of love or attachment to his family and friends, community or country, and is free from the psychological imperfections of selfish desires for name, fame, wealth or for anything, he can become a *Sanyāsin* and live on the charity of persons around him, who look upon him as an ideal or a perfect man and as an example for their own lives. The *Sanyāsin* is a man who has come back to the world from his quietude of retirement preparatory to spending the rest of his life in doing disinterested good to his fellowmen. He is now a citizen of the world of humanity and is therefore an ideal for all men.

This fourth *Āśrama* of the *Sanyāsin* is an institution for the Hindus. The *Sanyāsins* are their holy men and prophets and examples of what a human being can make of himself in terms of his freedom from wants and desires of any kind. In terms of wantlessness, contentment, and a serene realization of the unity of life with the rest of the creation, he is supposed to be the highest of men. These *Sanyāsins, Sādhus,* or *Swāmīs* are still respected in India. In fact, no one has a greater hold on the minds of men than these wandering mendicants, although, of the very large number of such men today, hardly a dozen are qualified to be worthy of this respect. This is the last and the final ideal of what a man ought to become, spiritually and morally, if he is not to die without having risen above the sensuous level of living. People are expected to see that no holy man is ever in need of shelter or his daily ration of food. This explains why millions of persons in India even without requisite moral or spiritual qualifications are still flourishing today under the titles of *Swāmī* and *Sādhu.* In no other culture or religion, could we have found so many millions of human beings living with perfect respectability or prestige without working for their livelihood. The idea of the four stages of life with the *Sannyāsa* as the highest stage, is a unique contribution of the Hindu religion and philosophy to the ideals of human life. The institution of the *Āśramas* which is supposed to be ideal and eternal in form, in the course of centuries, has degenerated into its mere outer form, devoid of the high spirit behind it. But it still exploits the traditional respect of the people for the *Sanyāsin,* or the renouncer, giving rise today to a large class of persons who are no better than worthless beggars. Now that the country is independent, the evil will disappear within the course of time, but one wonders if the good in it, namely, the ideal of a morally, spiritually, perfectly free and unattached man, will also not disappear with it.

The Four Varnas

We now come to the *Varnas*, or the fourfold classification of society into the *Brāhmanas*, the *Ksatriyas*, the *Vaiśyas*, and the *Śūdras*. The real significance of the classification does not lie in the historical fact of its being propounded by the Hindus of India more than twenty centuries ago, or its being practiced today in the extremely outdated form of the caste system. It lies in the fact that the Hindus evolved a structure of an ideal society, which must always include these four classes distinguished on the basis of their merits, qualifications, and functions. It is further contended by the Hindus that any society even today has these four classes. First, the elite or the learned, the wise or the leaders, the policy-makers, the lawgivers, the legislators are called today by the name of the rulers or the administrators. Second is the class of the defenders of the faith of the society called the military. They do not have to be either learned or wise as do the rulers. As fighters for the faith whenever it is in danger, they must only follow the policies and the dictates of the rulers. Third is the large class of traders, businessmen or merchants whose function is to produce and distribute consumer goods and wealth to the community and the people. Last, we have the largest class of people in the society who are not the rulers, the military men, or the business magnates, but are simply workers, laborers, wage earners. These correspond today to the Hindu *Varnas*, only we do not prescribe the same qualifications for their functions. But there are these four classes, *Brāhmanas*, *Ksatriyas*, *Vaiśyas*, and *Śūdras*. No society can work satisfactorily without the coordination of these four classes. Never will a society have only one or two classes as the Communists believe. The only difference between the Hindu classification of an ideal social structure and today's classification lies perhaps in the qualifications and duties of the *Brāhmanas*, or the good and wise men, who are the rulers of the society. This Hindu classification is not at all undemocratic when it is remembered that democracy does not mean that everyone is equally fit to be a *Brāhmin*. Originally this classification was based strictly on qualifications and merit and not on birth or heredity. As the centuries passed, classes based on occupations multiplied into hundreds, and, as occupation in olden times was based on heredity, the institution gave rise to the present caste system in Hindu society. As beggary is the evil legacy of the Hindu doctrine of the four *Āśramas* and gives the highest place in society to the begging *Sanyāsin*, the caste system is the legacy of the ideal fourfold classification of society which degenerated into a heredity-based structure. Both these institutions have a lot of ideal and rational thought behind them, and it is hoped that very soon, the Hindus may evolve a society based on its original and valuable pattern of an ideal individual life and an ideal social structure, exemplifying the principle of only the good and the wise, guided by the principles of the *Dharma* and *Ahimsa,* ruling the society.

Hinduism and Hindu Philosophy

There is a serious confusion in the minds of outsiders and some uninformed Indians, too, that Hinduism and Hindu philosophy are one and the same thing or that the latter is drawn from the former. Nothing can be more erroneous. The two are as poles apart as Christianity is from Western philosophy. The reflections of Plato and Aristotle, Locke, Descartes, Berkeley, logical positivism, the philosophy of analysis and phenomenology, and scientism have not concerned themselves at all with themes of Christianity. What is, one wonders, common between the Christianity of churches and the entire range of philosophical literature in the West. This parallels the case of Hinduism and Hindu philosophy. Hindu philosophy has taken an absolutely independent course from the earliest times of Sankhya and Yoga, Buddhism and Jainism to the Nyaya, Vedanta and Vaisesika, and has dealt with the problems of mind of all kinds, from absolute monism to pluralism, materialism to absolute idealism, from the distinctions between the universal and the particular, and finally the problems of relation itself. Hinduism has nothing at all to do with these hairsplitting problems of philosophy as Christianity has nothing to do with the problems with which Bradley and Bosanquit occupied their lives. Hinduism is a code of conduct based upon the concept of Hindu Dharma. With that go certain social institutions like Varna and Asrama Dharma sects for the attainment of *Moksa* (liberation) by *Bhakti* (devotion), or the worship of Siva and Visnu, or by *Jnana* (knowledge), or *Karma Margas* (action paths). Hinduism believes in immortality, transmigration of soul from body to body for innumerable years. Belief in God is universally held. All these matters are hardly dealt with either intensely or exclusively in any one of the major Indian philosophical schools or in the standard philosophical texts. Like Christianity, Hinduism is a set of beliefs, all unproven assumptions for the everyday man, but known to a few enlightened men of the age.

It is true that among Christians a great divergence has taken place on the question of revelation. Not many Christians today believe in the possibility of revelation, at least exclusive revelation. On this point there is quite a difference between Christianity and Christian philosophy. Not so between Hinduism and Hindu philosophy. In India, Hindus and Hindu philosophers alike have always believed in the revelatory character of the Vedas. But again, the tendency in India is increasingly in the Western direction, i.e., more and more Indians today regard the Vedas as only the earliest historical literature and strip it of its authoritative character of truth revealed for all times. It may be mentioned here that the term "Apaurseya," which is usually translated as "revealed in connection with the Vedas" has a different connotation. One of the great Indologists, Motilal Shastri, who was trained entirely in the traditional Hindu philosophy, has aptly clarified this fact. According to his research based on the Vedic and Brahmanic texts, the word "Apaurseya" means "concerned with eternal truths." Since the subject matter of cosmology and evolution covered in the Vedas is no one's personal property and is objective truth, the word "Apaurseya" is added to the knowledge concerning the area. I agree entirely with this interpretation.

The reasons for this confusion between Hinduism and Hindu philosophy are purely and exclusively historical. When the Muslim, the Western foreigner, the Portuguese, the Dutch, the French, and the British first came to India, their initial view was of the customs and manners, the religious practices, and the eating and bathing habits of the Hindus. All this had a religious tinge. Hindu religion, that is, Hinduism, therefore, came to be the first concern of the foreigners. There was for them no such thing as Hindu philosophy as epitomized in Sanskrit manuscripts. None of these Hindu philosophical texts were translated in any one of the foreign languages. Soon this religious phase was over, and some Europeans learned Sanskrit in India and translated just a few standard texts. This is the story of the last one hundred fifty years. Only now can the foreigner read in English very scanty selections from the Vedas, about ten or twelve Upanisads, and the six systems of Hindu philosophy. These standard systems of Hindu philosophy do not stand by themselves nor are they intelligible by themselves. There are hosts of commentaries to these texts without which the full flowering of Hindu philosophical tradition cannot be understood even today. I hope the United States, Europe, and India will increasingly take up the task of translating these commentaries into English. Hindu philosophy has taken an absolutely independent course of abstract reflection on almost all topics of interest to man, and in this technical character of its method, Hindu philosophy has nothing in common with Hindu religion and Hinduism.

The Jain Religion

The term Jain is derived from *Jina* meaning the victor, or the conqueror—implying conquest or final victory over the bondage of the ailments and ills of life. The ideal or the supreme purpose of Jainism is, therefore, the realization of the highest or the Absolute perfection of the nature of man, which in its original purity is free from all kinds of pain or bondage. Jainism does not consider it necessary to recognize any other perfect being besides man or any being more perfect than the perfect man. It is thus a religion of the perfect man. A being higher than the most perfect man is not considered necessary for either the creation of the world or the moral regulation of the universe. It is for this reason that Jainism is usually characterized as atheistic. But the term with its fixed connotation in Western thought, is likely to be misleading here. It is true that Jainism has no place for a god as a creator or a governor of the universe, and it would be more accurate to call it a heretical sect of the Vedic faith. Jainism had its origin in a revolt from the tradition and the authority of the Vedas. It is well known that among the early adherents of the Vedic faith, differences, in the course of time, arose on the question of animal sacrifice or the killing of animals for the sake of *Yajna.* The *Ahimsā Dharma* and its opposite had a theological tussle from the earliest time. And though the Jain tradition claims its faith to be eternal, it is more than likely that its earliest founders must have belonged to the sect that rebelled from the idea and practice of taking life. It is interesting to note that in the traditional line of the Vedas, those on the side of animal killing are all *Brāhmaṇas,* while the dissenters belong to the *Kshatriya,* or the warrior class, and that the perfect souls, or *Tirthānkaras,* of Jainism are all *Kshatriyas.* Jainism should, therefore, be characterized as a heretical sect of the Vedas, with predominantly monastic leanings, though its teachings are enjoined on all alike. Its peculiar genius lies in its emphasis on equal kindness toward all life, even toward the meanest. It is par excellence a religion of love and kindness.

HISTORY OF JAINISM

It has already been said that, according to the Jains, their faith is eternal, for *Ahimsā Dharma* is eternal. Time, which is infinite, is measured in cycles of evolution and dissolution called the *Utasarpaṇī* and *Avasarpaṇī* and each is divided again into six eras. It was in the fourth era of the second cycle that the twenty-four *Tirthānkaras* or perfect souls arose. These *Tirthānkaras* are supposed to have attained their perfection and absolute freedom from all bondage, and preached Jainism to the world. The first *Tirthānkara* was Riṣabha who was the real founder of Jainism. His name occurs in the Vedas and the Purāṇas also, but very little else is known about him. The last was Vardhamāna, otherwise known as Mahāvīra, who was also an elder contemporary of Lord Buddha. The following are the names of the *Tirthānkaras:* Riṣabha, Ajita, Sambhava, Abhinandan, Sumati Padmaprābhā, Supārsva, Chandraprabhā, Pushpadanta, Sitala, Sreyāṇśa, Vasupujya, Vimala, Ananta, Dharma, Śānti, Kunthu, Ara, Maltī, Munīsuvṛta, Nami, Nemi, Pārśva, and Vardhamāna.

This is the fifth era—with Mahāvīra ended the fourth era. Mahāvīra was indeed not only not the founder of Jainism, but actually comes last in the galaxy of his other well-known predecessors. His predecessor, Pārśvanātha, or the twenty-third *Tirthānkara,* is known to have died in 776 B.C. Neminātha, or the twenty-second *Tirthānkara,* is supposed to have preceded Pārśvanātha by some five thousand years. Contemporary research has made it unnecessary to refute any doubt regarding the existence of Jainism as an independent sect much earlier than either Hinduism or Buddhism. (See Dr. Jacobi's introduction to Sacred Books of the East, vols. 22 and 24 and works of other scholars.)

Lord Mahāvīra was born in 599 B.C. into the family of a ruling *Kshatriya* chief of the *Naya* clan. (The Buddhists call him *Nātaputra.)* He was born in the republic of Vaiśālī (Behar) at the site of the modern village of Basārh about twenty-seven miles north of Patna (the modern capital of Behar). After being a householder for about twenty-eight years during which time he had a daughter, he bade farewell to his family and retired to a life of solitude. Then he meditated upon the miseries of life and the means for final emancipation. After fourteen years he attained his objective, when he decided to preach Jainism. (It would be observed that his life history is almost parallel to that of the founder of Buddhism.) During the course of wide travels and wanderings, he preached for about thirty years and attained his final *Nirvāṇa* in 527 B.C. at Pāvāpurī (in modern Behar). Pāvāpurī has become, since then, one of the chief places of Jain pilgrimage. It is a small place in the midst of beautiful surroundings where a number of Jain temples have sprung up. *Diwali,* the annual day of the Hindu illumination, is the day of this pilgrimage. Lord Mahāvīra is supposed to have attained *Nirvāṇa* on this day. The main temple contains the sacred footmarks of Lord Mahāvīra.

THE SECTS OF JAINISM

Jainism is one and undivided so far as its philosophy is concerned. But a little earlier than the Christian era, the Jains began to split on the points of certain rules and regulations for the monks, and the two well-known sects, *Śvetāmbara,* or the white-clad, and the *Digāmbara,* or the sky-clad, were formed.

The points of difference between the two are just minor ones and are: that the *Digāmbaras* hold that a perfect saint goes without food; that he should own nothing, not even clothes, hence the practice of going naked; that salvation is not possible for women. The *Digāmbaras* have no nuns.

Later on, other minor sects called *Sthānakavādī* and *Lūnikās* were also formed, based on idol worship and similar matters. Not believing in a God, or *Avatars,* the Jains are not an idol-worshipping sect, but that has not prevented them from erecting and carving statues in honor of their *Siddhas,* or perfect souls.

CANONICAL LITERATURE OF JAINISM

The preaching of Jainism until long after Lord Mahāvīra, must have been by word of mouth, transmitted from generation to generation. The Jains relied entirely on memory for the propagation and preservation of their faith. They were also called *Nirgranthas,* or those having no books. It is generally believed that after the death of Mahāvīra, knowledge of Jainism as it was first preached gradually began to disappear, and it was only much later that it was again restored.

According to Śvetāmbaras, the canon was reduced to systematization by the council of Pātli-Putra about the end of the fourth century B.C. But it is generally agreed that it was given final shape only after eight hundred years, that is, in A.D. 454. (There is, however, some minor difference among scholars about the exact date.)

The systematized teaching of Mahāvīra consists of twelve *Aṅgās,* the last *Aṅga* being subdivided into fourteen *Pūrvas,* and five *Prakaraṇās,* along with other *sūtra* literature.

Among later works, mention should be made of *Lokaprakāsa,* an encyclopedia of Jainism, compiled by Vinaya-Vijai in A.D. 1652. Most of the canonical texts have now been published in India and English translations of at least seven of them are now available. The language of their canonical literature is *Ardha-Māgadhi,* a blend dialect of the province of Magadha (modern Behar), but it would be better to call it *Apabhramśa,* or *Jain-Prākṛt,* a corrupt form of Sanskrit. Jain literature has also contributed much towards the expansion and evolution of new forms of language. The above is according to the *Śvetāmbara* belief, however, the *Digāmbaras* hold that the entire literature was destroyed about A.D. 789. This carnage is ascribed to Śankarāchārya, the illustrious Vedantist, though no evidence exists for it. Some of the books, however, were saved in Nepal and in Śravanabelagol (in Mysore), the Jain headquarters of south India, and the second most important place of Jain pilgrimage where a colossal statue of Lord Gomteśvara exists.

JAIN METAPHYSICS

It would thus appear that the simple spirit of Jainism is not to be identified with the long vicissitude of Jain literature, for the Jain philosophy in its ultimate analysis is simplicity itself. It can be summarized in a few sentences. First, there are living beings; second, there is non-living matter; third, there is contact; fourth, as a result of these, there is a flow of karmic energy into the soul, causing in the *Jīva* the bondage of life and its experiences. And last, this inflow can be stopped which will result in the final *Mokṣa,* or liberation that is the ultimate goal or the aim of life. Jain metaphysics is thus a dualistic system dividing the universe into the two ultimate, eternal, and independent categories of the living and the non-living, that is, the *Jīva* and the *Ajīva.* Besides the *Jīva,* the other substances are the five kinds of *Ajīvas: Pudgala,* or matter; *Dharma,* or movement; *Adharma,* or rest; *Akāśa,* or space; and *Kāla,* or time. We have thus the six *Dravyas,* or the substances of Jainism. The soul which is always mixed up with matter except at the highest stage, is further subdivided into mobile and immobile, for even trees and stones are supposed to have souls. The soul possesses nine qualities in all, of which consciousness, or *Cetanā,* is the chief quality. Souls are also classified according to the number of sense organs they possess. Man possesses five senses along with the mind; the lower animals progressively scale down from five to one sense organ. About both soul and matter, Jainism adopts the common-sense view of their being innumerable. Their metaphysical system is thus pluralistic also. The soul is regarded as an active principle as distinguished from the mere knower of Sānkhya-Yoga system. The powers of the soul are limitless, and its striving for perfection is continuous. There being no power higher than that of the soul, the entire scientific and material progress of the world is but an infinitesimally small expression of the latent powers of the soul. Souls are again divided into those that have attained perfection, or *Mukta,* and those that are still in bondage and are struggling for freedom, or *Baddha.* Of the former, there are five classes, the *Pañcaparameṡthina,* or the five Lords of Jainism, ranked in order of merit, the two foremost being the *Siddha* and the *Arhat.*

As Jainism is a system designed primarily for the attainment of the perfection of the soul, it would be interesting to know what, by virtue of this achievement, a perfect soul is supposed to acquire. Every *Tirthānkara* is a perfect soul and acquires the following ten qualities:

1. averts famine in an area of eight hundred miles radius;
2. remains raised above the ground whether walking, standing or sitting;
3. seems to be facing everyone in all the four directions;
4. destroys all destructive impulses in persons around him,
5. is entirely immune from all possibility of pain and disturbances of any kind;
6. is able to live without food;
7. possesses mastery of all arts and sciences;
8. nails and hair do not grow;
9. eyes are always open, lids do not wink;
10. his body does not cast shadow.

In addition to these, he enjoys the four attributes of infinite perception, infinite knowledge, infinite power, and infinite bliss. These perfect souls are of two kinds—those with bodies and those without bodies.

Of the five *Ajīvas,* those of space, time, and matter are concepts common to other systems of thought. But *Dharma* and *Adharma* are the two most peculiar concepts of Jain philosophy. No other system of thought has anything like it. Unfortunately, the term *Dharma* has a variety of meanings in Hindu and Buddhist thought and the Jain concepts of *Dharma* and *Adharma* are unlike these accepted meanings. Exposition of the Jain concept of *Dharma* and *Adharma* has, therefore, naturally suffered from this confusion. But in itself the idea is quite plain. By *Dharma* and *Adharma* are meant the principles of movement and rest. A principle of movement has to be conceived as an uncreated and eternal substance, otherwise, it would be impossible to explain the universe. They do not mean "that which moves," but rather a condition providing for movement and rest, that is, if a substance had the principle of movement in itself, they provide the necessary condition for it. Besides the two categories of *Jīva* and *Ajīva,* the six substances are further classified from a different standpoint, as being either *Astikāya* or *Nāstikāya. Asti* means existence, and *Kāya* means volume or magnitude, technically called the *Pradeśa.* Except for *Kāla* all other substances including the *Jiva* are *Astikāyas.* Time alone has no *Pradeśa.* There are thus five *Astikāyas.* Thus, while on one hand, the classification of categories is on the basis of the life and no-life principle, on the other hand, it is on the basis of their possessing *Kāya,* or magnitude.

The next most important concept of the Jains is that of *Karma* and the karmic matter. As regards *Karma,* in common with other Indian systems, Jainism holds that every effect has a cause. *Karma* is that general energy of the soul which is the cause of its attachment with matter and its subsequent defilement. It is the link of union between the soul and the body. Since a God has no place in Jainism, *Karma* comes to occupy a very important position, indeed, in this system, for most of the functions of God are appropriated by the soul and its potential power. Connected with the doctrine of *Karma,* are the doctrines of reincarnation and transmigration which are also held. There is no shortcut to life's perfection, the Law of *Karma* being inexorable. Any idea of divine grace or forgiveness is, according to Jainism, only an oversimplification of the problems of sin, suffering and redemption, for a *Karma* can be destroyed only by another *Karma.* Jainism, therefore, specializes in an elaborate classification of the kinds and qualities of *Karma.* There are eight kinds of *Karma,* and as many as 148 of its subdivisions. *Karma* takes its start from the contact of the living and non-living, which is responsible for a flow of the karmic matter into the soul. This inflow attains fruition in the course of time; and, by a reverse process, this inflow and fruition are to be stopped, and the *Karmas* finally extinguished. Technically, this function of the *Karma* from beginning to end is marked by five stages: *Aśrava,* or inflow of *Karma; Bandha,* or bondage; *Samvara,* or fruition; *Nirjarā,* or stoppage; and *Mokṣa,* or liberation. Jainism works out a very imposing psychological superstructure of the spiritual destiny of man from start to finish. The Jains believe in five bodies or sheaths of the soul instead of the three or four bodies of the other systems. As the *Karmas* are destroyed bit by bit, the body acquires new qualities shedding its grosser manifestations; and as the bodies perish one after the other in the soul's ultimate march towards perfection, it passes through fourteen well-marked spiritual stages, the *Guṇasthānas.*

In summary, there are the two ultimate categories of *Jīva* and *Ajīva,* the six substances (one *Jīva* and five *Ajīvas),* the five stages of *Karma* with the two ultimate categories *(Tattvas,* or principles); and finally, if merit and demerit *(Pāpa* and *Puṇya)* are added to these seven principles, we have the nine *Padārthas* of Jainism. These are the fundamental principles of Jain metaphysics. Some critics of Jain metaphysics have found fault with this kind of cross division implying that the Jains had no clear concept of how many substances they really believed in. But such a criticism is founded on a lack of understanding, although Jain metaphysics is not very clear about the process of the creation of this actual world from these eternal categories and substances. This may be regarded as a weak thread in its metaphysics.

JAIN ETHICS

Jain ethics is a direct consequence of the Jain philosophy of soul and *Karma.* Since the primary duty of man is the evolution and perfection of his soul as well as of his fellow creatures, the principle of *Ahimsā,* or "non-hurting" of life irrespective of its distinction into higher and lower, is the cardinal principle of Jain ethics. Even the principle of truth may be sacrificed for the principle of *Ahimsā.* "Hurt no one" is a positive injunction enjoining love and compassion toward all fellow creatures. Jains alone build asylums and resthouses where old and diseased animals are kept and fed until they die a natural death. With a view to attainment of its cherished goal of *Mokṣa* by humanity as a whole, Jainism prescribes perhaps the most elaborate rules for practical everyday conduct. *Samyag Chāritra,* or right conduct, must follow *Samyag Darshan,* or right faith, and *Samyag Jyāna,* or right knowledge, and these three form the "three jewels," or the *triratna,* of Jainism.

Jain ethics is the most glorious part of Jainism. In one respect, it is quite simple, as the primary duty of man is the strict observance of the principle of *Ahimsā.* But, in another respect, it is anything but simple. For the rules of conduct prescribed are perhaps the most elaborate and complicated. Even in the guidance of the practice of *Ahimsā,* cruelty is analyzed into as many as nine categories, each subtler than the other. The number of rules to be observed in everyday life are too many and their discipline and rigor are about the hardest. Life is divided into a number of stages according to the evolution of the soul and a great many vows, such as, non-killing, non-stealing, chastity, non-possession, and daily worship, have to be taken even at its earliest stages. These rules of conduct are for all classes of persons, the ascetic as well as for the householder, and are much stricter for the former than for the latter. But as there is no conflict recognized between the true interest of the individual and humanity, it cannot be denied that even these rules are not without great social value. And since no ideal short of the absolute and perfect happiness of all living beings is conceived, Jainism, in a way, may be regarded as a bold and daring forerunner of modern theories of utilitarianism, which, in comparison, strike as but pale and feeble attempts at evolution of only a limited variety of humanitarianism. Criticism is often made of the impracticability of the exalted ideal of Jainism, but no one has set limits to practicability except Man himself.

JAIN LOGIC

The most distinctive contribution of Jainism is in the realm of logic and lies in its doctrine of *Naya,* which means point of view. According to Jainism, the Buddhistic doctrine of change and of nothingness was contrary to facts, and so was the Advaitic theory of absolute identity. Their foremost logical position, therefore, is what is called *Anekāntavāda,* or the theory of many-sidedness. It can be one thing and different when seen from different standpoints. It is obvious that about anything it can be said that it exists or does not exist with equal truth from different points of view. Again, from another point of view, the predication of both existence and non-existence can be made, while, from yet another standpoint, it can be said that the thing is indescribable. If we combine the last standpoint with the first three, we have all seven *Nayas,* or or points of view about a thing. That is why the Jains like to prefix every proposition with *Syād,* or maybe. Thus, the following would be the seven *Nayas:*

1. *Syād Asti*—Maybe, it is.
2. *Syād Nāsti*—Maybe, it is not.

3. *Syād Asti Nāsti*—Maybe, it is and it is not.
4. *Syād Avaktavya*—Maybe, it is inexpressible.
5. *Syād Asti Ca Avaktavya*—Maybe, it is and it is inexpressible.
6. *Syād Nāsti Ca Avaktavya*—Maybe, it is not and is inexpressible.
7. *Syād Asti Nāsti Ca Avaktavya*—Maybe, it is and it is not and it is inexpressible.

It is from these seven modes of expression that the theory derives the much-reputed name of *Saptabhaṅgīnaya.* While the modes of expression number seven, knowledge, according to Jainism, is of five kinds: *Mati,* or the ordinary perceptual knowledge; *Śruti,* or the scriptual knowledge; *Avadhi,* or clairvoyant knowledge; *Manaḥ-parayāya,* or telepathic knowledge; and, finally *Kevala jyāna,* or the absolute knowledge. The Jain doctrine of *Anekānta-vāda* is a unique contribution. In the realm of conduct, it preaches love and respect of all living beings; in the realm of thought, it affirms only relative or conditional validity to all propositions. No judgment, according to Jainism, is absolutely false, as none is absolutely true.

PRESENT POSITION

Jainism, like Hinduism, after stagnating for centuries petrified itself into sheer ritualistic and formalistic practices. After the spirit had left, the body continued to be artificially fed by blind adherence to dead formulae, until toward the end of the nineteenth century, India had a general awakening of the cultural and religious glory of its past. A wave of renewed enthusiasm for acquaintance with and study of its forgotten sources of inspiration swept the educated and the sensitive; and Jainism also shared in this revival, though not to the same extent. Jain Sacred Text Societies were formed, which discovered, edited, and published authentic texts. Young Men's Jain Associations sprang up in the north and the south of India, and a number of Jain gazettes and periodicals began to be issued. With a view to reform and propagation, a large number of popular books have also been written by able scholars in the various languages of the country. It is true that Jainism has no economic or political plan for the world, since it does not think in terms of multiplication or complication of the physical needs of man. Although it is indifferent to the forms of government, as long as it is in spirit a Jain government, that is, inspired by the unconditional love and respect for life, Jainism has not been neglectful of the educational and cultural betterment of mankind. While Jain literature and scholarship, both religious and secular, are themselves of no ordinary status, they have also taken due share in the development of arts in the country. They erected monumental *Stupas,* gateways, umbrellas, and pillars in honor of their saints. In the richness and quality of their architecture or carving in stone, Jainism would have few parallels in the world. Excellent examples of these exist in Junagadh, Osmanabad, and in Girnar. While Mount Abu in Rajputana "carries to its highest perfection the Indian genius for the invention of graceful patterns and their application to the decoration of masonry," Satrunjaya is one of the "loveliest temple-cities in the world." In the realm of religion and philosophical outlook, it preaches universal tolerance. Jainism sees no reason for wrangling among religions and faiths. Like Hinduism, it is a non-proselytizing faith and enjoins on its followers the same respect for a different faith which it has for its own. This aspect of Jainism is worthy of greater attention than it has hitherto received at the hands of its admirers and critics. Its attitude towards other forms of religion is that of perfect non-criticism. Jainism is not competitive, and has not, at all, cared for the spread of its faith. Its followers hardly totalled 1,500,000 in 1941. It has already been said that the message of Jainism is for all humanity. Its love extends not only to humanity but to all living creatures; and, shorn of its handicap of an utterly unsuitable rigidity of its ritualistic observances, the growth of *Ahimsā,* or the "spirit of Jainism," should have a great future and a great message indeed for a world today torn with growing hostility and uncontrollable violence.

REFERENCES

U. D. Barodia, *History and Literature of Jainism* (Bombay, 1909).
J. Burgess's edition of Buhler's *On the Indian Sect of the Jainas* (London, 1903).
Jagmandar Lal Jaini, *Outlines of Jainism* (Cambridge University Press, 1940).
H. L. Jhaveri, *First Principles of Jain Philosophy* (London, 1910).
A. B. Lathe, *An Introduction to Jainism* (Bombay, 1905).
Margaret Stevenson, *The Heart of Jainism* (Oxford and London, 1915).
H. Warren, *Jainism* (Madras, 1912).

Some Riddles in the Behavior of Gods and Sages in the Epics and Purāṇas

Ever since my school days when I began to read the Indian epics and the Purāṇas in Hindi, I have been puzzled by what appears to me to be far too numerous instances of the indefensible behavior of our most honored sages and saints in these classic sources. I have also wondered why my countrymen, by and large, have not attended to this aspect of these hallowed stories which are known by the majority of the literate and the illiterate Hindus in our country and have also been proudly repeated by our elders to their children for thousands of years.

So far as the readers and listeners of these stories are concerned, a possible explanation does come to mind. The Hindus with regard to this particular aspect of the subject matter have suffered and are still suffering from a psychological disability called scotoma. This consists of a sighted man never seeing what he does not want to see. For example, if my mother, who has wonderful eyes, should happen to hang in her prayer room a picture of Siva and Parvati actually in the act of coitus, no amount of effort on my part would succeed in showing it to her. She sees only Siva and Parvati in the picture and is simply unable to see anything else. But the problem still remains, the problem is on the part of the writers of these stories. Why would they write and publicize such gross sides of their own moral and spiritual sages and saints?

In this chapter I propose the following questions, and I would like to know which answer, if any, satisfies the demands of either the ancient or the modern Hindu mind. Are the few accounts cited below true in detail or are they all untrue? Should they not be deleted or declared to be shameful lies interpolated by unscrupulous writers or narrators in the past? Should these stories about Indian sages and saints be allowed to disfigure the pages of otherwise highly respectful sources of our moral and spiritual heritage? Can any other sense, if any, be made out of them? Was the moral tone of sexual abstinence never, after all, as real in India as it is depicted to be? So far, I have known of only two kinds of reactions to the narration of such stories. The first is of Swami Dayananda, the founder of Arya Samaja and a great scholar of the Sanskrit heritage of India. In his opinion, all such references to the behavior of Indian gods and sages deserve to be burnt and destroyed. However, he does not attend to the question as to how and when they came to be written at all. But the Sanatan Dharmists will not listen to Swami Dayananda's interpretation. I think the burden lies on the traditional Hindus to try to explain and make sense of these. The other reaction with which I am familiar is that of the late Principal N. V. Thadani of Delhi, who did not regard the epics of the Purāṇas as realistic or historical accounts and tried to explain the entire and vast bulk of this literature as allegorical, and symbolically embodying the eternal truths of Indian philosophy and religion. For him, semen, incest, coitus, reckless pleasure in destroying virginity, anger, and curses do not stand for the ordinary and conventional meanings of these terms, but have quite a different and a consistent philosophical meaning with regard to religious content. Obviously none of these explanations are quite satisfactory.

INCEST

It is rather surprising, especially in contrast to the generally idealistic and highly spiritual interpretation which is so strong in India, to find that actions which are ordinarily considered in violation of all moral standards and the standards of even common decency sometimes are found in some of the more sacred text of the Indian religious tradition, and pertain to the behaviors of our ideal types of men and women. The compatibility of these practices, including the use of supernatural powers for worldly and immoral practices, seems to be somewhat commonplace and apparently accepted without any challenge, denunciation, or even moral compunction on the part of the perpetrators of these views. It is interesting to note some of these unusual and as it were inexplicable situations. They pose riddles to the serious minded and pose moral problems to those who are deeply concerned in this area of behavior.

The Vedic hymns are said to contain references to incestuous relations. Agni is said to impregnate his own mother. In the same Saṁhitā, and elsewhere, is described the incestuous relation of Prajāpati with his daughter. The twin gods Asvinas—the children of Savitṛ and Usas—married their sister Surya. Pusan loved his sister. The famous dialogue between Yama and Yami refers to a brother-sister love affair.[1] The Aitareya-Brāhamaṇa also refers to incestuous relations between the mother and son.[2]

Sarkar, taking his stand on the dialogue between Yama and Yami, the episode of Prajāpati's incest with his daughter as narrated in the Brāhamaṇas and in the Vedas, maintains that incestuous relations between brother and sister, father and daughter, as well as between mother and son were not uncommon. But why should great saints and sages indulge in these? And how, ethically, can they?

UNCONTROLLED SEXUAL PASSION

Vyāsa, the legendary compiler of the great epic was himself progeny of unwed love. His mother, Matsyagandha, as the epic narrates, was the foster daughter of a fisherman, and she rowed her father's ferry boat from one shore of the Ganges to the other. Once, sage Parasara happened to be a passenger on her ferry boat. The fair fisherwoman attracted the attention of the sage at once, and soon a desire to enjoy her arose in his mind. He accordingly expressed his desire. Matsyagandha refused him on the plea that she was ashamed of cohabiting in public with so many people on both shores looking upon them. But the sage at once created a mist round the boat so that nobody could see them. Wonderstruck at this miracle, the maiden spoke again, "Know me to be a maiden, O brilliant one, under the protection of my father. My maidenhood would lapse by your contact; how, then, shall I be able to return home? I shall not be able to stay at my father's house hereafter. Consider all this first, and then act as you like." The girl was relieved of her fear by a promise on the part of the sage that her maidenhood would be restored to her after intercourse. The sage further undertook to grant Matsyagandha any boon she cared to ask. Accordingly, Matsyagandha expressed the desire that a sweet perfume emanate from her body. The sage granted it, and the intercourse between the two took place on the boat. As a result of the union, Matsyagandha, now also known as Yojanagandha because of the pleasing odor emanating for miles around from her body, at once gave birth to a child called Dvaipayana whom she cast off on an island (Dvipa).[3] In the same Parva when Matsyagandha (as Satyavati) narrates this episode to Bhisma, she says that she agreed to the proposal of Parasara because she was afraid of a curse if she refused him. She also states that the child born out of the union was cast off by her on the island as the sage instructed so that she might be a virgin again.

When Kunti was still a young girl and was staying with her foster father Kunti-Bhoja, she was entrusted with the task of receiving guests and treating them well. Surya loved her and declared: "Neither your father, nor your mother, nor any of your elders have any right over you" (I. 99, 9-12). He also said that a woman was free to behave as she liked. He demolished the fears of Kunti by telling her that after intercourse she would regain her virginity and that the son born of the union would be very famous (III. 291, 12-16). In due time, she gave birth to the mighty Karna bedecked at birth with armor and earrings as was promised by Surya; but, due to the fear of her kinsfolk, she put Karna in a chest and floated the chest onto the Ganges. And none but an old nurse knew the secret (III. 292, 2-6).

The *Mahābhārata* narrates the legend of the adulterous intercourse of Indra—a mighty god—with the wife of the sage Gautama. The story of the illicit love between Ahalya and Indra is very old and one of the oldest Brāhamaṇas, namely, the Satapatha, addresses Indra as Ahalya's lover (III. 3, 4, 18). Once Indra disguised himself as Gautama and approached Ahalya saying, "You are in your *ṛtu* (mating season). Let me cohabit with you." Ahalya recognized Indra, but consented to his proposal out of curiosity. When she was fully satisfied, she said, "I am now fully satisfied, so please go away quickly and protect yourself, as well as me, from Gautama."

King Pratipa was approached by the river goddess Ganga for the satisfaction of her sexual desire. She occupied the right side of his lap and requested the king to satisfy her passion.

The *Mahābhārata* also refers to Śvetaketu, who begot a son by the wife of his preceptor (XII. 35, 22).

In a dialogue between Astavakra and Disa, the latter exposed her sex in the following way, "O *Brāhmana,* a woman loves the pleasure derived from senses even more than the gods like Vayu, Agni, and Varuna, because they are by nature lustful" (XIII. 19, 91-94).

A long legend is narrated about how Vipula by supernatural powers protected his preceptor's wife from the amorous advances of Indra (XIII. 40, 14).

Galava was facing a dilemma when Madhavi herself found a way out of this. She told Galava that a *brāhman* learned in the Vedas had given her a boon according to which after each delivery she would be a virgin again.

In all these episodes the virginity of the girl is restored after intercourse takes place, and one mysterious explanation or another is given as to how this happens. Thus, a virgin married her brother, stayed with him for the night, and still "the lovely one with the glorious waist, the very mighty one, at the end of each day became a maiden again."

Vyāsa is repeatedly addressed as the son of Parasara, and Karna as the son of Surya and not of Pandu.

A legend narrated in the *Anusasana-parva* reminds us of the influence of the tradition according to which the mighty god Varuna abducts the wife of a *brāhman.* In this legend both the abductor and the abducted woman were not punished by the husband of the woman. Bhadra, Candra's daughter, was given away in marriage to Utathya, because he was very handsome and was also approved by Bhadra herself. The god Varuna wanted the girl for himself. So, once, when Utathya was out, he went to the forest regions of Yamuna and carried away Bhadra to his own underwater mansions, and enjoyed her there (I. 78).

The god Varuna is not questioned or punished for his enforced intercourse with Bhadra. Varuna, the upholder of morality, himself carries away the unprotected wife of a *brāhman* ascetic without the least compunction.

CURSING

In the epics both *brāhmans* and ascetics, are found to be the most short-tempered people. On finding the slightest breach in conduct or on the inflicting of the pettiest insult a person in cursed. As a matter of fact, the story of the *Mahābhārata* starts from a curse inflicted upon King Pariksita for disturbing a sage's penance. Similarly, Pandu is cursed because he unknowingly kills a sage who in the form of a deer was enjoying the sexual act. Cyavana, enraged at Sukanya's playful activity, curses her father with a curse which stopped the excretory function of the men in his army. Even a small impudence on the part of a king who did not give way to sage Śakti, who was a *brāhman* and had a right over the road, invited a curse. King Lomapada refused to give a *brāhman* something and because of that it did not rain in his kingdom for twelve years and all his subjects suffered along with the king who had actually committed the offense. Sage Jaratkaru abandoned his wife at a slight offense, her offense being a reminder to perform his daily duties. Uttunka cursed King Pausya for serving him food with a hair in it. The idiosyncracies of Durvasa, whose marked characteristic were a short temper and cursing, are well known.

While denouncing anger so often and so sharply, the epics declare: "The wrath of a *brāhman* is like a fire which burns not only the offender but also his family."

Poison in the form of a *brāhman's* wrath is even more deadly than that of a black serpent, because there is no remedy for it (XIII. 159, 33).

The Vana-parva of the *Mahābhārata* declares, "Great is the anger of the great-souled ones, and great is also their favor. It was the wrath of a *brāhmana* that made the waters of the ocean salt. Fire in the form of the wrath of the sages of the Dandaka forest is still burning and does not die out. Much is heard about the powers of such great *brāhmanas*" (III. 197, 24-27).

Once the daughter of King Tṛnabindu accidently entered the hermitage of a sage and thereupon became a prey to his curse. Returning to her father, she reported the physical change she had undergone. Her father approached the sage immediately and requested him to marry the girl. He did so gladly, and later a son was born.

We find Yudhisthira cursing his mother because of the ill treatment she gave to Karna. "From now onward, no woman will be able to keep a secret" (XII. 6, 10).

Miraculous powers and the ability to curse were the two weapons that the *brāhmans* utilized so frequently.

Curses are flung at simple actions, even those done unknowingly. This is apparent from the instances of Dasaratha, who is cursed for his unintentional murder of Sravana; Karna, who is cursed for unknowingly killing a cow; and Pandu, who is cursed for killing a sage in the disguise of a deer.

Visvamitra, who by a severe penance tried to become a *brāhman,* lamented his short temper when he cursed the apsara Rambha sent by Indra to guide him.[4]

The *brāhman* Kausika repents his rash action of burning a bird to ashes because of anger (III. 197, 5-6, 31-42).

We come across numerous incidents in the *Mahābhārata* describing cases of various sages ejaculating their semen at the sight of beautiful damsels or *apsaras.* The seed, being that of a mighty king or of a refulgent sage, never goes to waste; it is reared somehow and a great sage, a strong hero, or sometimes a very beautiful maiden, is born from it.

How can these rather astounding activities be explained or made compatible with what one might expect of gods and sages? Are these actions in violation of rules which should be followed, or are they to be looked at as transcending the whole realm of moral rules? Are they to be looked upon as "legitimate" actions of persons possessed of supernatural powers, or are they to be interpreted as the actions of persons who misuse these powers or who have sunk back into the realm of ordinary human beings with all the temptations of the physical body? How can they be explained? How are they to be explained? How are they to be judged? They are not denied, and so the "riddles" seem to persist.

NOTES

1. Rgveda, V. 3, 3; Rgveda, X. 61, 5-7; Atharvaveda III. 6, 7. For other reference to father-daughter incest see S. C. Sarkar, *Some Aspects of the Earliest Social History of India,* pp. 137-138 (Rgveda, VI. 55, 5; X. 21, 8).
2. Aitareya-Brāhmaṇa (VII. 13, 9-10).
3. Mahābhārata, I. 51-56; Mbh, I. 57-58; Mbh, I. 57, 61-62; Mbh, I. 57, 63. All numbers in parentheses throughout the chapter refer to the *Mahābhārata.*
4. Ramayana Balakanda, 64. 17; also cf., Sundarakanda, 55. 3-6.

Autobiography of a Yogi

Autobiography of a Yogi as a title for a book sounded strange indeed to my Indian ears—for it is not traditional for a yogī in India to speak of himself as such, nor does a spiritual man call himself by the highest title "Paramhansa," which is reserved for only those rare souls who have attained their liberation from the bondage of earthly life and activity and live in complete equanimity of mind *(samādhi)*. (Not even Swami Vivekananda called himself or was ever referred to as "Paramhansa.") I draw the attention of the reader to these technical inaccuracies, because in spiritual matters they are not only misleading to the public but actually harmful to the spiritual aspirant himself.

Autobiography of a Yogi is an astonishing book and was probably written from a combination of motives, from the legitimate one of self-advertisement to the noble one of acquainting a foreign reader with the supernatural power of the spiritual forces over the physical world, believed to have been possessed by the yogīs in India. But, unfortunately, this autobiography focuses the attention of the reader on just those aspects of spiritual life and yoga which for ages have been regarded as hindrances in the path of a yogī's relization of God. Other persons, therefore, who claim to know India and respect her for her spiritual achievements in the past and the present, may be forgiven if they do not regard God-realization and yoga as Swami Yogananda does.

To review specifically the contents of this autobiography of forty-eight chapters would be only a repetition. The reader is merely led from chapter to chapter in a narrative of miraculous occurrences, the majority of which happen to the author himself, or to which the author was witness. If we assume them all to be authentic, they produce an impression that the essence of a spiritual or divine life has centered around supernatural powers and their exercise—which in some cases call upon God to satisfy almost any whim of man. The miracles described are too numerous to mention here. They occur to the Swami from his infancy to his arrival in America, and range from personal and spontaneous wish-fulfillment to the resurrection of the dead. It is surprising to note that almost all the miraculous occurrences take place in India, before the Swami's arrival on American soil. While scores of these were crowded into the Swami's pre-American life, scarcely one miracle has occurred during his twenty years in America. Is it that materialistic America is not yet ready for miracles, even from an Indian yogi? Almost every chapter deals with a miracle, but a few chapter titles selected at random may give an idea of the content of the book: The Saint with Two Bodies; A "Perfume Saint" Performs His Wonders; The Tiger Swami; The Levitating Saint; The Sleepless Saint; Outwitting the Stars; A Mohammedan Wonder-Worker; My Guru Appears Simultaneously in Calcutta and Serampore; Kashi, Reborn and Rediscovered; Rama Is Raised from the Dead; Materializing a Palace in the Himalayas.

There also lurks a subtle method in the chronological recounting of such miracles (pp. 100, passim). The only three chapters free from the miracles are the ones on J. C. Bose (the famous Indian scientist), Rabindranath Tagore, and Mohandas Gandhi. There is absolutely no connection between these chapters and the rest of the book. The reader has no option but to think that they serve only the egocentric purpose of associating the Swami's name with Bose, Tagore, and Gandhi. But this is somewhat incongruous, for, happily, the lives, personalities, and work of men like Gandhi and Tagore (whom most religious and spiritually minded men follow and respect) are supremely free from the powers that fill the pages of this autobiography. The book on the whole leaves the reader with the impression that it would have been much better had the author followed what he himself says: "Performances of miracles ... are spectacular, but spiritually useless. Having little purpose beyond entertainment, they are digressions from a serious search for God" (p. 50).

The book, widely advertised and read, will no doubt acquaint the reader with India, yoga, and Swami Yogananda, but whether it will portray them truly is quite doubtful. Truth never suffers so much from its opponent as from its overzealous devotee.

Jainism

Jainism is a religion of India whose ideal is the realization of the highest perfection of the nature of man, which, it holds, was in its original purity free from all pain and the bondage of life and death. The term Jain is derived from Sanskrit *jina* (victor, conqueror) and implies conquest over this bondage, which is imposed by the phenomenal world. Jainism does not consider it necessary to recognize any higher being other than the perfect man, and for this reason it is usually said to be atheistic. It can also be called a heretical sect of the Vedic faith, which had its origin in revolt from the tradition and the authority of the Vedas; its earliest founders may have belonged to the sect that rebelled from the idea and practice of taking life prevalent in the Vedic animal sacrifice. Jainism as a religion has predominantly monastic leanings, though its teachings are enjoined on all alike. Its peculiar genius lies in its emphasis on equal kindness toward all life, even toward all life, even toward the meanest; it is par excellence a religion of love and kindness.

Jainism has never been torn by philosophic dispute, but in the 4th or 3rd century B.C. the Jains began to split into two sects on points of rules and regulations for monks, a rift which was complete at least by the end of the 1st century A.D.

The Digambara (sky-clad, naked) hold that a saint should own nothing, not even clothes; hence the practice of going naked. They also believe that salvation is not possible for women. The Shvetambara (white-clad) differ from them on all these points.

LITERATURE

According to the Shvetambara, the sacred literature preserved orally since Mahavira was systematized and written down by the council at Pataliputra (Patna) about the end of the 4th century

B.C., but it is generally agreed that it was not given its present shape until some 800 years later (about A.D. 454). It consists of 12 *angas* (sections), the last of which is subdivided into 14 *purvas* (former texts) and 5 *prakaranas,* along with other *sutra* (aphoristic) literature. Among later works, mention may be made of Lokaprakasha, an encyclopaedia of Jainism compiled by Vinaya-Vijai in A.D. 1652.

The Digambaras hold that the entire literature was destroyed about A.D. 789. Some of the books, however, were saved in Nepal and in Sravana Belgola (in Mysore), the Jain headquarters of south India (and the second most important place of Jain pilgrimage, where a colossal statue of Lord Gommateshvara exists). The language of their canonical literature was originally Ardha-Magadhi, a blend dialect of the province of Magadha (modern Bihar), but as the texts are largely rewritten it would be better to call it Apabhramsha or Jain-Prakrit, a corrupt form of Sanskrit. From at least the 9th century, Jain texts were also written in Kanarese.

PHILOSOPHY

Jain metaphysics is a dualistic system dividing the universe into two ultimate and independent categories: living beings or souls *(jivas),* which permeate natural forces such as wind and fire as well as plants, animals and human beings; and non-living entities *(ajivas),* which include space, time and matter.

The next most important concept is that of *karma,* a subtle invisible substance composed from one of the types of matter, which flows into and clogs the *jiva,* causing the bondage of life and transmigration. This inflow can be stopped by many lives of penance and disciplined conduct, resulting in the final *moksha,* or liberation, the ultimate goal of human endeavor. Karmic matter is elaborately classified according to its effect: for instance, one type is that which prevents true knowledge; another, that which causes pleasure or pain. Since no god has a place in Jainism, *karma* comes to occupy a very central position, for most of the functions of a god are appropriated by the soul and its potential power. Souls are divided into those that have attained perfection and those still in bondage. Of the former there are five classes in order of merit, the five Lords of Jainism.

ETHICS

The Jain ethic is a direct consequence of the philosophy of soul and *karma.* Since the primary duty of man is the evolution and perfection of his soul and that of his fellow creatures, *ahimsa,* or nonhurting of life, irrespective of its distinction into higher and lower, is the cardinal principle. "Hurt no one" is a positive injunction enjoining love and compassion toward all creatures; Jains alone build asylums and rest houses for old and diseased animals, where they are kept and fed until they die a natural death. The three ideals of *Samyag-Darsha* (right faith), *Samyag-Jyana* (right knowledge), and *Samyag-Charitra* (right conduct) are known as the three jewels, or the *triratna.*

Jainism also prescribes most elaborate rules for everyday conduct; for example, for guidance in the practice of *ahimsa,* cruelty is analyzed into as many as nine kinds, each subtler than the last.

LOGIC

A distinctive contribution of Jainism lies in its doctrine of *naya,* which means "point of view." According to Jainism, the Buddhist doctrine of change and of nothingness, which postulates that all things are transitory, was contrary to facts, and so was the Advaitic theory of absolute identity. Their foremost logical position is what is called *Anekantavada,* or the theory of many-sidedness of reality and truth.

ART AND ARCHITECTURE

Not believing in a god or *avataras* (incarnations of a god) the Jains are necessarily not an idol-worshiping sect, but this has not prevented them from erecting and carving statues in honor of their *siddhas,* or perfect souls. They have erected monumental *stupas* (hemispherical domes of solid masonry, surrounded by railings with ceremonial gateways and surmounted by an umbrella) in honor of their saints, and the richness and quality of their architecture and carving in stone have few equals. Excellent examples exist in Junagadh, Osmanabad and Girnar (just east of Junagadh, Saurashtra), while Mt. Abu in Rajasthan represents in its highest perfection the Indian genius for graceful masonry decoration. Satrunjaya (near Palitana, Saurashtra) is one of the world's most beautiful temple cities.

POSITION IN THE 20TH CENTURY

Jainism preaches universal tolerance, and its attitude toward other forms of religion is that of noncriticism; it is not competitive and has never cared for the spread of its faith. Its followers totaled just over 1,600,000 in the early 1960s, with the Digambara majority in the south and the Shvetambaras in the north. Among its followers are found the rich traders and merchants of Gujarat and Maharastra, forming about 0.45 percent of the total population of India.

REFERENCES

S. C. Ghosal, ed., *The Sacred Books of the Jainas* (1917).
Hermann Jacobi, trans., *Gaina Sutras,* Sacred Books of the East, Vol. XXII and Vol. XLV (Oxford: Clarendon Press, 1884, 1895).
Margaret Stevenson, *The Heart of Jainism* (Oxford and London, 1915).
J. Jaini, *Outlines of Jainism* (1915).

Svapramanatva and Svaprakaṣatva: An Inconsistency in Kumārila's Philosophy

The Mīmāṅsā is noted for its unusual view of the authoritativeness and the validity of all cognitions as such. The view is taken from the Jaimini Sūtra 1, 2, and 5, and is developed by both Kumārila and Prabhākara in their respective works of Ślokavārtika and Bṛhati. Kumārila expounds the view in Ślokavārtikā Sūtra 2, in which it is maintained that all cognitions as soon as, and when, they arise are inherently endowed with validity. Thus, starting from the supposition of an inherent quality of truth of the cognitions, what is to be established by subsequent investigation is not their truth but their falsity. The question is asked, wherein can the truth of a cognition lie? It can lie either in its own self or outside itself, i.e., in the excellence of the sense organs, etc. But if the truth of a cognition did not belong to the cognitions and depended upon external conditions, one would have to wait for the actual experiences of life till the ascertainment of their truth by an examination of the external causes of the alleged discrepancy has been established.

Let us take an example. If a man with the intention to write perceives a pen and picks it up, he does so under the assumption of a belief in the validity of his perception. In other words, his cognition is its own 'Pramāṇa'. The 'Pramāṇatva' of the cognition comes from within itself, 'Svataḥ'. No one after seeing a pen ordinarily broods: "Let me think if this perception of mine is valid, for it may be invalid. Are my senses in perfectly excellent condition and are other circumstances of cognition favorable to a valid perception? Am I sure that it is only a pen I have just seen and no other object, etc.?" If such was the normal procedure of thought after perception, all practical activity of life would become paralyzed. But such, however, is not the case, and this establishes the Self-validity of our cognitions. And therefore only those cogni-

A paper read at the Philosophical Congress held at Hyderabad in December 1939.

tions are false which either are due to defects in our sense organs or are later on sublated. But all other cognitions are *ipso facto* true.[1]

Kumārila goes on to add that if cognitions did not have this 'Sakti' of self-validity, nothing could produce it in them. If the validity of a cognition is made to depend upon conditions other than itself, the process would lead to an infinite regress without establishing the validity of cognition at all. Hence the 'Svataḥ-prāmāṇyan' of all cognitions. While in other systems of epistemology, it is the truth of a cognition which has to be ascertained, in Mīmāṅsā epistemology on the contrary, it is their falsity which has to be established. The validity of an apprehension cannot come from outside 'parataḥ,' and even when a cognition is later on sublated and disproved, it only disproves the validity that originally belonged to the previous cognition. If validity did not already belong to the previous cognition, it could not later on be set aside.

The question now is, how is this theory of the 'Svataḥpramāṇatva,' i.e., the intrinsic validity of cognitions related to the 'Svataḥ-prakāṣatva' or the intrinsic cognizability of cognitions. It seems reasonably clear that the two theories mutually imply one another and are complementary, if not actually identical. To say that a cognition is inherently valid is only to say that it is self-luminous. 'Svataḥpramāṇatva' means only 'Svataḥjnanatva.' Just as when one has perceived an object, he does not doubt that he has perceived that object, similarly, one does not doubt that when he has cognized he has cognized an object; the reason being, that in both cases, cognition or awareness carries its own revelation along with itself. If cognitions were not self-luminous and had to depend for their own cognizability upon other conditions, then their intrinsic validity too, could not be immediately and directly established. In fact, the concept of the intrinsic validity of cognition presupposes the intrinsic cognizability of cognitions, if any distinction at all can be made between the two concepts of 'Svataḥpramāṇatva' and 'Svatāḥprakāṣatva.'

One looks in vain for anything more than the self-luminosity in the concept of self-validity. Self-validity hardly means anything more than self-cognizability, which is the same as Dharma-Kīrti's famous assertion that if one does not believe in the cognition as directly cognized, one could not establish the cognition of anything. Besides, almost the very same argument of infinite regress and the impossibility of apprehension apply against the theory of non-self-luminosity of cognitions which are advanced against the extrinsic validity of cognitions. Our point is that hardly any difference of importance can be made between the two concepts of 'Svataḥpramāṇatva' and 'Svaprakāṣatva.'

Yet strangely enough, Kumārila who advocates the theory of 'Svataḥpramāṇatva,' in Sūtra II of his 'Ślokavārtikā later on turns out to be an opponent of the theory of self-luminosity of cognitions later in the 'Suryavāda' of the same Vārtikā. His criticism of self-illuminancy of cognitions is unsatisfactory, halfhearted, and unspirited. No serious argument is advanced except the analogy that cognition is like the light in the eye which only illumines other objects but not itself. Just as it is not in the power of the eye to illumine itself, so is the case with cognitions also.

We have considered in detail elsewhere the inappropriateness of the analogy of the eye and the cognition and have also shown the difficulties of a theory of non-self-luminosity.[2] The point here is to consider if one can reasonably hold the theory of the intrinsic validity of cognitions and in the same breath deny the theory of intrinsic cognizability of cognitions.

It seems clear that what is not intrinsically cognized cannot be established as intrinsically valid also, for, what is dependent for its cognizability upon later cognitions and inferences, cannot guarantee its own validity which can then be only extrinsic, and due to external conditions. If the intrinsic validity of cognitions is to be admitted, in order to avoid an infinite regress, the same must also be the case with the intrinsic cognition of cognitions. Kumārila admits that if validity did not belong to the cognitions inherently and intrinsically, validity could not be stamped on the cognitions from outside. Exactly the same must be said with regard to cognizability too. If cognizability did not belong to the cognitions intrinsically and inherently at the very first stage, it could not at any later stage be added to it.

Cognitions are either cognized or uncognized, and if they are cognized, it is far more satisfactory to hold that they are immediately cognized than subsequently cognized. We cannot maintain the view that cognitions are uncognized, for in the first place, it would be absurd to maintain that objects are cognized without the cognition being cognized, and secondly, all systems of thought agree in holding that the cognitions *are* cognized by *some* means and at *some* stage.

If the above analysis of the relationship of the two concepts of the self-cognizability, and self-validity is correct, the question is, why did Kumārila contradict himself? It seems that Kumārila has been inadvertently led to a criticism of 'Svaprakāsa vāda' in his chapter on 'Suryavāda' by the force of an overpowering anxiety to combat the 'Vijnānavāda' theory of the essential sameness of the subject and the object of knowledge. It is generally feared that the concept of self-illuminancy of consciousness on the theory of immediate perception, if established, would add weight to the subjectivist theory of 'Vijnānavāda.' Therefore, Kumārila, like most anti-subjectivists, is anxious to maintain an absolute externality, independence, and otherness of the world of objects as against the theory of the objects being only a form of the inner subjective series of cognitions. As against the subjectivist Vijnānāvādi, who does not make any absolute distinction between the subjective and the objective, it is thought necessary to uphold that the two separate worlds of the inner cognitions, and the outer objects, never do fuse into each other, or appear indifferently both as subjective states and as outer objects. His forces of mind are something like this: To admit that cognitions are self-luminous is to admit that an object can be both a subject and an object, and to admit this, is to play the game of the subjectivists, ergo, cognitions cannot be self-cognized.

Kumārila, therefore, maintains that nothing can be both a subject and an object and that the two functions of the knower and the known cannot belong to one and the same cognition. Cognition therefore cannot be self-cognized, because a wide gulf between the knower and the known must at all cost be maintained in order to combat the subjectivist. Cognitions cannot be admitted to be their own objects whatever may be the consequences of a theory of cognition by another cognition or by inference.

Thus, pressed by the need to maintain an absolute distinction of the internal states of cognitions and the external world of objects, as against the solipsist, Kumārila forgets what he had previously propounded in his second sūtra, pressed under a similar need of maintaining the immediate and the intrinsic validity of the Vedic injunction. He obviously thought that without the theory of an intrinsic validity of cognitions, the inherent authoritativeness of the Vedas could not be maintained. But in his zeal to demolish completely the subjective idealism, he overshot the mark by attacking the 'Svatāḥprākāṣatva' of cognitions, not seeing the inconsistency in it with his own earlier position.

It is a little difficult to see why, in order to restore the objectivity of our cognitions against the subjectivists, it should be considered obligatory to deny self-cognizability of cognitions. Yet the practice has been fairly common with some philosophers, in spite of the repeated declaration that by the theory of the 'Svatāḥprākāṣatva' of cognitions is not meant that either cognitions do not have an extra-mental basis, or that cognitions are their one subject and the object. On the contrary, a theory of self-luminosity of cognition is perfectly compatible with the belief in the fullest externality of the object of cognition as shown by Saṅkara, who retains both the self-luminosity as well as the objectivity of cognitions and yields to none in his opposition to the 'Vijnānavada' subjectivist. To say that cognitions are grasped immediately and simultaneously along with the objects cognized is not to say that cognitions and their extra-mental substratum are identical, which is the conclusion feared by the anti-subjectivist. Nor to say that cognitions are self-luminous is to maintain with the Buddhist 'Vijnānavāda' his theory of the non-reality of objects apart from the cognitions. Yet the two contentions above have often been unfortunately confused and taken as necessarily implying one another, and philosophers with the exception of Śaṅkara and Prabhākara, have not taken pains to separate the two distinct issues of the self-cognizability of cognitions and of an absolute subjectivity of cognitions. The former, as an epistemological problem is far narrower in scope than the latter problem of the ontological status of objects. The epistemological doctrine of the self-cognizability of cognitions can in no way be identified with a metaphysical doctrine of the mental solipsism of reality.

Kumārila is therefore inconsistent, for either the cognitions are not intrinsically valid or they are also intrinsically cognizable. He cannot have it both ways, namely, retain 'Svaparamāṇatva' and destroy 'Svaprakāṣatva,' for the two notions stand or fall together. It is refreshing to note in this connection that Prabhākara, who fully shares with Kumārila his theory of the self-validity of cognitions as well as his opposition to the subjectivist Vijnānavāda, consistently maintains, unlike Kumārila, the theory of the self-luminosity of cognitions.

NOTES

1. S.V. Sūtra II.
2. Shri Krishna Saksena, *Nature of Consciousness in Hindu Philosophy.* (Banaras: Nand Kishore and Sons, 1944).

The Nature of Buddhi according to Sankhya-Yoga

According to dualism both consciousness and unconsciousness exist independently and eternally as perfect opposites, and yet they somehow are related. As long as they stand isolated and unrelated, there is no experience which arises out of a failure to realize the unrelated nature and the Kevala existence of the Cit. The moment this unrelatedness is realized, there follows the liberation, or the Kaivalya, of the Puruṣa which is the goal of experience. But if, as the sutra says,[1] that experience is failure to distinguish the Sattva and the self which are absolutely unmingled, the question naturally arises how does experience start if originally the conscious Puruṣa is not in contact with the unintelligent Prakṛti and if the two are Atyantāsaṅkirṇa. Vācaspati puts the question thus: How can the self, whose essence is intelligence and whose brightness does not depend upon another, be properly said to illumine that which is inert, and on the other hand, how can the inert *take* illumination?[2]

The answer to the above question and an explanation of the possibility of experience is thought to be provided by a theory of reflection or double reflection, based upon the transparent nature of the Sattva.[3] It is said that the Sattva, although not in combination with the intelligence, but insofar as, being absolutely clear, contains the image of the intelligence; it seems to come in contact with intelligence and so experiences the various things.[4] This is illustrated by the statement, "Buddheh prati samvedi puruṣa," i.e., the Puruṣa, who is not a direct seer and who knows by reflecting the concepts of the Buddhi, is said to be a knower. It is, of course, assumed in order to make the association of the Puruṣa and the Sattva possible, that the Puruṣa is not absolutely different from the Sattva. "Sa buddher nātyantam virūpah."[5] The Puruṣa is not absolutely different from the Buddhi for though pure, it sees the ideas after they have come into the mind. It cognizes the phenomena of consciousness after these ideas have been formed, and though its nature differs from the phenomena, it appears to be the same. Consciousness, therefore, according to this dualistic standpoint arises either out of a supposed transcendental and single reflection of the Puruṣa in the Sattva as held by Vācaspati or out of a mutual reflection of the one upon the other as held by Vijñānabhiksu.[6]

To put it briefly, the process would be like this. The Buddhi suffers a modification according to the form of an object it cognizes, and having assumed the form of an object has to come in contact with the constant factor, the Puruṣa, or the eternal light. Out of the contact of these two, there arises the illumination in the Buddhi in the form of "I know this" which is reflected back in the Puruṣa (which confuses this state belonging to the Buddhi as belonging to Puruṣa), or having reflected his light on the Buddhi, Puruṣa regards himself as his own reflection. The same is meant by Pratyayānupasyah. The inactive Puruṣa erroneously regards himself as active in perception owing to the reflection of the active Buddhi in it, and the unconscious Buddhi seems to be conscious owing to its proximity to the conscious Puruṣa.[7]

But in an account of knowledge and experience presented above, there is a serious difficulty. It is said that the Cit, which unites not with the object, is conscious of its own Buddhi when it takes its form by reflecting it.[8] But how can the Cit take the form of the Buddhi without itself conforming to the fluctuations of the mind? The answer is that "Although the moon does not unite with the clear water still it *seems* to unite with it insofar as its reflection unites with the water. Similarly in this case also."[9] Although Cit does not unite with the Buddhi, it seems to unite since its reflection has united with Buddhi. But, how can even a seeming reflection of the Puruṣa arise in the non-intelligent Sattva, or the ever unmodifiable Cit take upon itself the changing character or knowledge? An answer to this question is sought in to be extracted from *Yoga-Sūtra,*[10] which shows that the pure nature of the Buddhi has something in common with the Puruṣa. In the Kaivalya state, Buddhi can be so pure as to reflect the Puruṣa as truly as he in himself really is. But the theory of the hypothesis of the purity of the Sattva and its resemblance to the Cit, which is supposed to enable it to catch a glimpse of the Puruṣa, either damages the strict dualism of the position or does not explain reflection. For Puruṣa is so altogether different from the Buddhi that there is hardly a common meeting point between it, which is Trigunatita, and the Sattva which is one of the Guṇas.

We do not therefore have a satisfactory explanation of knowledge in the dualistic theory of Sānkhya-Yoga, according to which the unconscious Buddhi is suddenly and mechanically illuminated by the Puruṣa. It first of all assumes that the subject and the object of experience are wholly outside experience and then struggles to bring them inside. As Sri Radhakrishnan says: "If the passive consciousness of the Puruṣa and the incessant movement of Prakṛti are regarded as independent of each other the problem of philosophy is insoluble."[11] An analysis of experience should be able to tell us that the subject and the object of knowledge are not absolutely separate and that equally both have a fundamental transcendental consciousness as their support within which they unite.

CRITICISM OF THE THEORY OF THE INTERMEDIARY NATURE OF BUDDHI

In Sānkhya-Yoga metaphysics any relationship between consciousness and unconsciousness seems absolutely impossible.

But some recent Indian scholars (Dasgupta and Sinha) have tried to reduce the gulf between the Puruṣa and Prakṛti and to make an interaction of the two possible on the basis of which alone is any supposed reflection to take place. It is obvious that a reflection between two absolutely heterogeneous objects is not possible. Attempts therefore have been made to reduce the antithesis to its minimum by providing for the similarity of the Sattva in its purest state with the nature of the Cit and thus making an interaction possible.

Professor Sinha says, "The dualism of Sānkhya is modified by the admission that there are different grades of existence among the modifications of Prakṛti, the highest of which is Buddhi."[12] The Buddhi is unconscious no doubt, but it is so transparent owing to the predominance of the Sattva that it is not entirely foreign to the nature of the Puruṣa, hence, it can catch the reflection of the Puruṣa, whereas gross material objects cannot reflect the light of the Puruṣa owing to the predominance of Tamas in them. Thus Buddhi is represented as a kind of "intermediary reality between gross matter and conscious Puruṣa,"[13] and is supposed to partake of the nature of both. It is unconscious like gross matter, but it is transparent like self-luminous Puruṣa. It is only in the Buddhi that the conscious Puruṣa and the unconscious material objects come into contact with each other. Thus there is made possible a mutual reflection of the one in the other.

According to Professor Dasgupta, "The ordinary difficulty, as to how entirely dissimilar wholes can come into contact with each other vanishes when we look at the point from Sānkhya-Yoga perspective."[14]

These interpreters perhaps take their stand on such statements as, "He is not homogeneous nor entirely heterogeneous"[15] and "Sattva purusayoh suddhi sāmye kaivalyam,"[16] where an attempt is made to bridge the gulf and make experience possible on a theory of the similarity of the Puruṣa and the Sattva. But the question is, does the attempt succeed? Buddhi may be pure and transparent by the predominance of Sattva in it, it may also be the highest evolute of Prakṛti, but that does not make it lose its character of being on the other side of the rigidly bifurcated reality. The subtlest and the finest evolute of Prakṛti is after all Prakṛti, and it cannot become identical with or share the nature of Puruṣa. If Puruṣa and Prakṛti meet in Sattva, as is supposed above, the dualism of Sānkhya-Yoga is virtually given up. The "physical and the mental may be the modifications of the same ultimate real," namely Pradhāna, yet they are not the modifications of the other ultimate reality, the Puruṣa, who is ever unmodified. Professor Dasgupta contradicts himself without realizing the contradiction when elsewhere he say that Buddhi, Ahankāra, and Manas, though psychical entities, do not belong to the Puruṣa; they are all stages in the evolution of the Prakṛti.

Does he mean that an evolution of Prakṛti when it becomes very pure and transparent becomes Puruṣa? The Sattva is either a constituent of the Guṇas (no matter how fine) and must be completely unlike the Puruṣa and incapable of any contact and reflection, or if it can take any reflection, it gives a lie to rigid dualism. If Sattva can become so fine and transparent as to be able to catch the reflection of Puruṣa, nothing prevents Sattva from becoming one with Puruṣa. One step more and Prakṛti and Puruṣa are ontologically one and the dualism is merged in monism. Such an easy solution of the difficulty confuses transparency with Cit. All Cit is transparent, but the converse is not true; the transparency of the crystal, the shining metals, and the water is not the same as intelligence. Partial resemblance cannot be stretched into perfect identity; otherwise Buddhi in the Kaivalya state would be identical with Puruṣa. The Sānkhya Kārikā definitely says that the dancer stops dancing after final separation is realized.[17]

So long as Buddhi is utterly different from Puruṣa, it does not improve matters to make it an intermediary or a hyper-physical entity. The problem of Sānkhya-Yoga is not only to make possible a contact of the two but to make it possible on their professed antithesis. A more logical position is to give up the attempt as impossible or the metaphysics of dualism as untenable.

Professor Dasgupta concludes: "So the relation of mind and body is no special problem in the Yoga theory." One would have thought that is was obvious that in the system of Yoga both body and mind of the Western philosophy were the evolute of the same ultimate real, namely, the Pradhāna, and that the question was not of the relation of the mind and the body, but the question in Yoga philosophy was of the relation of the mind and the Puruṣa. The dualism in Yoga is not between mind and matter, but between mind and Puruṣa, a kind of transcendental dualism between transcendental and empirical consciousness.[18]

Dualism of Sānkhya-Yoga and the possibility of experience cannot coexist, and to make Buddhi share the nature of both is more to give up the dualism than to solve a problem from the professed platform of absolute difference between Puruṣa and Prakṛti.

NOTES

1. *Yoga-Sūtra,* 3.35.
2. Vaisāradi on *Yoga-Sūtra,* 3.35.
3. As to how exactly the two, Puruṣa and the Sattva, meet to enable experience to take place, there is significant divergence between the opinions of Vācaspati and Vijñānabhiksu. According to the former, the reflection is a single affair, i.e., the Puruṣa is reflected in Buddhi just as a face is reflected in a mirror, or, moon in water. There is no further or mutual reflection of the mirror in the face or the reflected water in the moon. Thus on this hypothesis, the Puruṣa remains unmodified. Vijñānabhiksu, on the other hand thinks that this single reflection would not be able to explain experience or knowledge. He therefore suggests that on Puruṣa's being reflected, it is this mutual reflection which enables Puruṣa to take cognizance of the modifications of the Buddhi, thus confusing the experience of the Buddhi as its own. Both these explanations are prone to difficulties. While the later better explains the possibilities of experience, it compromises the true and transcendental nature of the Puruṣa. The former, while it ill explains the possibility of experience retains the original purity of the absolutely unmodifiable nature of the Citsakti. See Index I, also Y. Vārttika on 1.4 and 3.35.
4. *Yoga-Sūtra,* Vaisāradi, 2.17.
5. *Yoga-Sūtra,* 1.4 and 3.35.
6. *Yoga-Bhāśya,* 2.20. See Index II.
7. *Sānkhya-Pravacana Bhāśya,* 1.87.99.104 and *Yoga-Sūtra,* 1.4.2.20.
8. *Yoga-Sūtra,* 4.22.

9. Vaisārdi on 2.20 and 4.22.
10. *Yoga-Sūtra,* 3.55.
11. *Indian Philosophy,* Vol. II, p. 332.
12. Sinha, "Indian Psychology," p. 125.
13. Sinha, "Indian Psychology," p. 125. According to Sānkhya, Buddhi is an intermediary reality between gross matter and the conscious Puruṣa.
14. Dasgupta, *Cultural Heritage of India,* Vol. 1, p. 407.
15. *Yoga-Bhāśya,* 2.20.
16. *Yoga-Sūtra,* 3.55.
17. *Sānkhya Kārika,* 61.
18. *Yoga-Sūtra,* 2.6.

The Individual in Social Thought and Practice in India

When an individual is given the same freedom which any other individual may claim for himself, he is treated as an individual and is given the rights of individuality. Another way to stress the same point is by the use of the concept of ends and means. If an individual is treated as an end in himself—in terms of equality of freedom and status—and never as a means to another individual's purposes, he is then considered a genuine individual.

But this kind of individualism is a purely abstract and atomistic individualism, on which alone no society can be based, and practically all social philosophies recognize this fact, in India as elsewhere. Expressions of pure individuality are always suspect in all societies. All sane societies put a limit to individualism in the interests of social welfare and other values which alone make individualism respectable. About India through the ages one fact stands out prominently. It is this highest regard for such over-individual ends through which alone an individual is supposed to live his life in society and be a significant individual. But this does not mean that the rights of an individual are thereby disregarded.

It has been superficially assumed by some observers that the Indian[1] social set-up itself is anti-individualistic, that in Indian social thought and structure there is too much authoritarianism, that not all men are regarded as individuals having equal rights in themselves, that the right of underprivileged persons to improve their individual social status is denied to them. In spite of the fact that such anti-individualistic practices have existed at times in India, the whole spirit of Indian social thought and structure originating from the most ancient times of the Vedas up to the present time has accorded due regard to individuals as individuals. All efforts of social theorists have been directed in India, not only toward the betterment of the individual, but also toward the opportunity of every individual ultimately and finally to attain his social destination. Society exists for the sake of the individual, and the social heroes in India have always revolted against discriminating practices. India has always tried to accord social equality to all individuals, though with little success during its dark ages.

Indian tradition has always been tied in intellectual and emotional admiration only to individuals who created and molded the society. The heroes in the Indian social mind are all individuals—sages and saints—and not schools or "isms" or ideologies. The Indian mind traditionally does not bother about ideologies or "isms" as such. It allows them all to coexist and has a genuine tolerance toward all ideological diversities. Rāma, Kṛṣṇa, the Buddha, hundreds of medieval saints, and such reformers in recent times as Tagore, Gandhi, Ram Mohan Roy, Ramakrishna, Aurobindo Ghosh, and Nehru are all prized as individuals. What is adored in social Hinduism or in any social period is not a historical social process as such, but a particular individual who has brought about social betterment; not the adoring of the age of Gandhi, but Gandhi himself.

It may be worth noting also that the recent linquistic wrangle among the different zones of India and even the traditional style of personal names are other interesting signs of individualism.

EARLY PERIOD

The history of the early Indian period reads like that of a modern and individualistic society wherein the standards of equality and of the freedom of the individual as an individual irrespective of any kind of discrimination are firmly established in theory and in practice. No differential treatment existed. Women had the same freedom and equality as men; there was absolutely no seclusion. Women sometimes had more education than men and had a prominent position in religious and social gatherings. Monogamy was the rule of life. Neither prohibition on remarriage of widows nor the evil of *satī* (the practice in which the wife immolates herself on her husband's funeral pyre) was known. This was a time in India when, according to Davies, "There was no woman question at Athens because all women were as mere vegetables, and there was no woman question at Sparta because both men and women there were little better than animals. Whereas in India, boys and girls underwent a ceremony of *upanayana,* or initiation, into education together."[2] Even much later we have the names of great women participating with men in religious and philosophical debates. It is well known that women were among the great Upaniṣadic philosophers. Men and women performed sacrifices together. There is not doubt in the minds of scholars and historians about the extreme liberality of attitudes toward all, including even fallen women and women captured in war. To die in defense of women was regarded as the surest way to heaven. Megasthenes, the great Greek historian, who was in India in about 300 B.C., has left a life-like picture of the Indian people. The Greek ambassador observed with admiration "the absence of slavery in India."[3] This is perhaps an exaggeration, because there was slavery of a kind in India during that period, although it was of an altogether different kind from that prevalent in other parts of the world during the same period.

There is positive evidence of equality among the different races that came to India from the outside in early times. The characteristic of the early Indians to absorb different social elements into a unity has been so predominant as to become one of the chief points of Indian culture. That there were marital relationships between these outsiders and Indians is also well known.

The Indian theory of *varṇa,* or classification of society into four classes, was in perfect conformity with then contemporary ideas of freedom and the status of the individual and social justice, and was and remains democratic with regard to the individual's status and his relation to society. It is supposed to be of divine origin, but this is not to be taken literally. It has purely ideological and functional bases and is universal inasmuch as society must have classes of individuals according to their qualifications, interests, and abilities to engage themselves toward the progress of society and toward their own fulfillment, religious or secular. This does not mean that the classification was static or immobile or that an individual, if he was endowed with ability and knowledge, could not attain to whatever classification he aspired.

In India the learned were recognized as the highest class, because only the wise can lead or lay down and perpetuate the faith for the people. They were called *brāhmaṇas,* who are supposed to give us the ideals and faith to live by. The *kṣatriyas* were second—they were the political and military leaders, who were supposed to defend the policies and ends of the social order. Third was the class of the wealth producers and distributors, called *vaiśyas.* The last class was that of the manual workers, craftsmen, and artisans, the *śūdras.* This classification was not based on heredity; birth had nothing to do with it. In their ideological functions there is to be found no fifth class, according to the

Mahābhārata and also the much-maligned Manu.[4] One's *varṇa* types is determined completely by one's actions, pursuits, and ideals. By man's own nature he falls into these four types.

While the first three classes are said to be twice-born, the fourth is said to be once-born, and therefore inferior. This means only that the members of the fourth class have not had the education and do not have the skill of the other three classes. These are persons who are only biologically born, but not born a second time by the training of education and culture. The qualities which are predominant in each one of the four classes are not exclusive of one another. The *Gītā* says that the four classes were established on the basis of *"guṇa,"* which means ability, and *"karma,"* which means actions or vocations.[5] The most sacred *Bhāgavata-purāṇa,* which is well known even by the illiterate, says "I consider *śvapaca* (literally, a dog), that is to say, the lowest class, whose mind, speech, activity, purpose, and life are fixed on the lotus feet of Viṣṇu (God), to be better than a learned *brāhmaṇa."*[6] "A person should be identified by the class whose characteristics he possesses even though that class is not his own by birth."[7] We read further, "By devotion a *śūdra* may attain the highest status."[8]

It is interesting to note that not only was Suta, the narrator of the *Bhāgavata-purāṇa,* himself born of the lowest class, but so were numerous spiritual and moral personalities who are regarded as teachers of the highest truths, such as Nārada, Prahlāda, etc. They were all men of low-class origin, a fact not very often stressed. Numerous lower-class men and women, such as hunters and even *caṇḍālas* (lowest in the social scale), have attained the abode of Viṣṇu. The *Bhāgavata,* which is the most representative of all the Purāṇas, does not at all depict the viewpoint of the later-established orthodox social or economic group. According to the *Bhāgavata,* the devotees of Viṣṇu should be free from all pride in their birth and should recognize no distinction between themselves and others. The main point of the teaching of the *Bhāgavata-purāṇa* is the absence of qualifications based on birth, etc.

The primary objective in the whole of India's extensive devotional literature is to refute the idea that a person's social status or class membership is of any significance at all. It is well known that the *gopīs,* the cowherd girls of the Kṛṣṇa *līlā* (play), are the primary examples of true devotion, despite their low-class status. The most singularly condemned in the *Bhāgavata-purāṇa* are the twice-born members of the three upper classes. In the Rāmāyaṇa, Rāma, the divine incarnation, ate berries previously tasted by Sabri, a woman of the lowest class *(bhīlinī).*[9] What is central is the the *Bhāgavata* does not acknowledge the superiority of even *brāhmaṇas* on the basis of their birth alone. The famous story of Satyakāma Jābāla in the *Chāndogya Upaniṣad* is refreshingly pertinent in this connection.[10] In the *Mahābhārata,* great warriors like Droṇa and Aśvatthāmā, etc., were all *brāhmaṇas.* In Vedic times, the *brāhmaṇas* were all agriculturalists. As a social practice, old persons—men and women—and the blind had precedence over kings and *brāhmaṇas.*

Dakṣa says, "One who desires happiness should look on another just as he looks upon himself."[11] Devala says that "the quintessence of *dharma* is that one should not do to others what would be disliked by oneself."[12] The same is repeated in the *Āpastamba-smṛti,* and in other *Smṛtis,* too. Mitākṣara remarks that *ahiṁsā,* or non-hurting, and other qualities are the *dharmas* (duties) common to all, even the *caṇḍālas.*[13] The *Mahābhārata* says that "for protecting a family, one individual may be abandoned; for protecting a town, the family may be abandoned; for protecting the society, the town may be abandoned; and for protecting the true self, even the world may be abandoned."[14] The great empire-builders of India, the Nandas, the Mauryas, and the Guptas, were all low-born. The Gupta emperors married *licchavis* (lower-class dynasty).

Young girls had a decisive voice in the selection of their husbands. On festive occasions and at tournaments girls appeared in all their gaiety. In the Vedic period, women did not suffer from any special disabilities. In the *Mahābhārata,* Śvetaketu's father says, "The women of all classes on earth are free."[15] A single standard for both men and women prevailed. Women were so sacred in India that even the common soldiery left them unmolested in the midst of slaughter and devastation. Wrote Dubois, "A Hindu woman can go anywhere alone, even in the most crowded places, and she need never fear the impertinent looks and jokes of idle loungers.... A house inhabited solely by women is a sanctuary which the most shameless libertine would not dream of violating."[16]

The refrain of the prayer in the *Mahābhārata* is not for the *brāhmaṇas* or for any special class of individuals. We read, "May all beings be happy, may all attain bliss...."[17] This emphasis on "*sarva,*" meaning "all," without distinction of caste, class, or creed, is typical of the Vedic and the Epic literature or periods. The *Āpastamba* declares that "there is nothing higher than the soul" and the *Śatapatha-brāhmaṇa* says, "None among souls is, on the whole, greater than any other soul."[18] Numerous quotations from other sacred literature can be adduced in support of similar social sentiments. When Nārada, a household name in Hindu society, lists the thirty features of the *sāmānya-dharma* (the duties of all the people), he specifically states that these are for all men. That is to say, they are not the *dharmas* of any particular group or class or caste of people, but are *sarva-dharma,* i.e., for all men. The *Manu-smṛti,* the Śānti-parva of the *Mahābhārata,* and the *Bhāgavata-purāṇa* abound in similar sentiments.[19]

Socially, in the Indian spirit all people have been regarded as different and separate individuals living their lives as different entities, responsible for their thoughts and practices, and expected to rely on their own efforts toward their betterment and ultimate liberation from bondage. The Indian doctrine of *karma* has had tremendous social effects on the Indian mind. Because of this law, an Indian regards himself as completely responsible for all his deeds. In fact, the Law of Karma is the greatest contribution of the Indian mind in having formulated a truly individualistic attitude vis-à-vis society. It is the most powerful social element of individualism in Hinduism and also in Buddhism. Everyone is exclusively and completely responsible for his or her actions and their consequences. No individual is saved or condemned by any force outside himself—in some schools, not even by God. The Law of Karma is an affirmation, in the strongest terms, of the principle of personal individuality and responsibility.

But, in spite of all this, the existence of slavery of some kind admits of no doubt. Emperor Aśoka (third century B.C.), when proclaiming his law of piety, enjoined that the law of piety consist in kind treatment of slaves and hired servants.[20] In the *Artha-śāstra,* Kauṭilya gives important kindly provisions about slaves.[21] Manu speaks of different kinds of slaves.[22] Malcolm writes that male slaves were "generally treated more like adopted children than menials."[23]

MEDIEVAL PERIOD

Such is the story of the status and dignity of the individual in India in relation to society for about two thousand years of its early history—in the basic and classical texts and in the life of the times. Then came a long period of what is known as India's Medieval Period. India lost its political status and unity. There was no one central authority to legislate for the Indian population as a whole. The country stood divided and separated into hundreds of local or regional kingdoms, all competing and vying with each other to keep their own powers intact. India lost its original spirit of freedom and free enterprise, its earlier outlook; it felt oppressed and driven to mere existence. All efforts centered on preserving its identity, allying all social customs and behavior completely to its religions, which remained the only common bond among the Indians.

Then the caste (as distinct from the *varṇa)* system of India became rigid. Enslaved Hindus, with no education or freedom of the spirit, found it easier to take up and grow in the profession of their fathers and forefathers. To try to do anything new, or to seek new careers, would have been not only too hazardous but practically impossible. All those professions which continued as hereditary became *jātis,* castes, and each caste took to social relationships between its own group in inter-dining and intermarrying. There came to exist some 3,000 castes based on occupation.

Along with this, it was natural that ideas of hierarchy were introduced. The *brāhmaṇas,* being responsible for religious ceremonies and the reciting of the sacred *mantras* (hymns) and being the only literate men, were still at the top, and at the bottom came the practitioners of the dirty work of cleaning the latrines or dealing with the skins of dead animals, etc. Since personal cleanliness was a surviving heritage, it gave rise to ideas of pollution and untouchability. The learned kept reading and studying ancient texts and copying manuscripts even in this age, but the people at large were practically living animals under their own religious beliefs, devoid of all spirit of dignity and of free inquiry and criticism.

The caste system, all sorts of discrimination, restrictions on widow marriage, forced *satī,* slavery, early marriage, etc., spread on grounds of sheer survival. These are not the social thoughts and practices of civilized India in its period of glory; these are the survivals of a dead India in itself unfree and slave.

CONTEMPORARY INDIA

The new India wants to eradicate these evils as quickly as possible. They do not represent the living India, which has come to breathe its own air again only recently, though India had always been looking backward to its earlier period, the *"Sat-Yuga,"* the period of truth, justice, and freedom. As India became a political unity and free once more after centuries of political slavery, her freedom of spirit revived. The evils of India are not representative or characteristic theories of the status of the individual in society, but abominations attempted, at a critical period, in defense of India's preservation. They have to be rooted out from Indian society in spite of the place they found in the Hindu Dharma-śāstras, which give only the record of a time and do not prescribe eternal truths or facts. Even orthodox Smṛti writers like Manu recognized that a time may come when their rules might become obsolete, and therefore declared that, if any rules framed by them are found to be not conducive to the welfare of society or against the spirit of the age, they should be unhesitatingly abrogated or modified.[24] As the famous Indian poet Kālidāsa says, "Nothing is good simply because it is ancient, and nothing is faulty merely because it is new."[25] The same sentiment is also expressed in the Śānti-parva of the *Mahābhārata.* The modern challenge to caste is by no means the first challenge it has encountered. The evils of caste have dogged India for centuries, to be sure, but they and the entire institution itself have been under repeated challenge and criticism. Over the centuries, long before the arrival of the British, new reform movements within India repeatedly attacked the caste system.

A religion on the defensive has to be reactionary, and consequently the growth of Hindu feeling at the time did not create conditions suitable for a reorganization of social life. The situation is different today. The Hindu feeling which has developed now is primarily secular and not religious. Today, there is no danger to Hinduism, and the urge for reorganization of society for the individual is there. It is expressed in the uprising of the lower classes and the unprivileged groups. The transfer of political power has provided the masses with the power to destroy social institutions based on privilege and on heredity. Social problems are being tackled from the point of view of a reawakened social conscience. The desire of the Indians to take their place with the progressive nations of the world, which is one of the major motivating forces in India today, has an urgency. It may be asked, if the variety of anti-individual customs which until now constituted the social structure of Hinduism have been destroyed or replaced, what will be left that will be characteristically or traditionally Hindu? The answer is that, except for the *varṇas* and the *āśramas* (stages of life), other social institutions of Hinduism are in no way integrally connected with the inner spirit of Hindu religion. No Hindu would argue that, if the joint family ceases to exist in the very near future or castes cease to operate as an institution, Hindu religious thought would be affected. (Incidentally, only 14 percent of families in India are of the extended type, and so the view that the joint family greatly lessens or denies the significance of the individual does not apply seriously to India as it apparently does to the Chinese and Japanese traditions and cultures.)

For a proper appreciation of Hinduism, with its basic principles of equality of opportunity and for *"loka-saṁgraha,"* or the common good, and for the perfection of man, it is necessary that it should not be confused with or infused by the social order of medieval times. The challenge of "modernism" that Indian society faces today is something which it never had to face before. It is the authority of the national state armed with legislative powers and motivated by a desire to bring Indian institutions in step with new ideas that is new today. Once this movement starts, it cannot stop. During the present transitional period, many Indians seem to live simultaneously in two worlds, the traditional, static, caste-bound, family-centered, and the new, Westernized, modernized, rationalistic world of dynamic individualism and social progress. This is probably inevitable, and it is not altogether bad, so long as the quite visible changes toward individualism inherent in industrialism and modernism hasten to destroy all remnants of social injustice.

To some, the economic planning of contemporary India indicates or implies an anti-individualistic program which is often interpreted as socialism. This is not an accurate picture even of contemporary India and surely not true to the Indian tradition in its economic life. Economic freedom in the sense of free and equal opportunity for all has been the essence of the Indian way of life throughout history, except during the Medieval Period. No one has been prevented from making his or her livelihood or seeking economic welfare and even accumulating money—almost in any way one pleases, provided, the books say, this is achieved without violating the rules of morality *(dharma).* There were no anti-individualistic curbs on the economic activities of the householder except *dharma.* As a matter of fact, the householder was praised by Manu as most important as being the supporter of society as a whole.[26] True, what did not exist in the earlier centuries—and to a certain extent recently—were the actual opportunities for attainment of financial security and economic accumulation. But the freedom for such opportunities was always recognized.

After the coming of freedom, India introduced a number of agricultural and land reforms for the betterment of the people as a whole. Landlordism, in which the great mass of individuals had practically no economic status, was abolished. A new movement for the consolidation of scattered and small holdings of individual farmers has been established. Also, the government has aided in providing mechanical tools, irrigation projects, and improved techniques. But little of this is actual socialism—the economic system of India is only partly socialistic—but, rather, development in the direction of social welfare for all the people. The so-called socialistic program of India's economic life does not deny individual opportunity, individual wealth, or individualistic economic justice, and is not in any way connected with any political ideology of an anti-individualistic nature.

The reforms that have been made have been directed against a lack of a sense of social welfare or social responsibility in India, and they do not have any destructive effect whatsoever upon the opportunity, the freedom of choice, or the right of economic pursuit by individuals. There has been some socialization or nationalization of industries which are vital to the country as a whole, but this has been indispensable in view of the unscrupulous attitudes and practices of many of the big industrialists and manufacturers and in the interest of social and economic justice for all.

These reforms have been based largely upon practical concerns. These economic and social monistic tendencies do not really find their bases in an alleged philosophical monism such as the Advaita Vedānta, which is only one extreme philosophical point of view and not typical of Indian metaphysics or any other Indian philosophical schools, as some are inclined to think.

CONCLUSION

Given the brief survey of the social ideas and practices of the Indians spreading over a three-age period of about three thousand years, the conclusions are three:

1. India has a glorious tradition of respect, freedom, and dignity of the individual, and the individual in relation to society—as glorious as any country has today. This ancient tradition of India was, of course, never purely individualistic. This was because of the religious and moral teachings of the Hindus and Buddhists, that the highest destiny of the individual lies in the perfection of his individuality in a way which inevitably takes him outside his narrow egoism and brings him fulfillment in relation to the society in which he lives. That is one reason why Hindu social structure provided for deep sanctity of social institutions such as the family, the school, the *varṇas,* and the four stages of life.

2. In Indian society the main concepts which governed the in-

dividual were those of his duties and obligations toward other individuals or something extra-individual. This is the reason the *rights* of the individual are not given a prominent place. Rights are there, but rights always carry obligations, and, if the concept of one's obligation is kept in the forefront of one's mind, society should be deemed (other things being equal) as giving a praiseworthy place to the individual and his relation to society. In terms of Indian thinking, no individual can be completely perfected if the core of his being lies merely in his insistence on his own rights. The rights of an individual are the minimum he should have and should not be deprived of. But no individual should be content with merely the minimum. He should rise above his rights and perfect himself by concentrating on his duties and obligations. The Indian emphasizes his qualifications or abilities rather than his rights. After all, it is one's qualification *(adhikāras)* that determine his rights. Without qualifications there are no rights. If an individual fails to perform his duties, he is deprived of his qualifications and rights.

3. Ever since India obtained the authority of legislating for itself as a nation, it has, in keeping with its past tradition, passed legislation against the practice of all obsolete and anti-individualistic practices between individuals and between society and the individual. Thus it has once again shown its ancient tradition of respect, dignity, and equality of all men. There are numerous working factors—such as the spread of education of both sexes, increasing industrial and economic opportunities, equality of the sexes, the example of socially advanced countries, and the urge of individuals and groups which have been discriminated against to catch up with the lapses of centuries—that make the Indian people hopeful that medieval undemocratic social practices will become a relic of history much sooner than has been achieved in any country in the past.

There are some modern writers who emphasize the inevitable cultural lag, the distance between the democratic laws enacted in present-day India and the actual social practices, and the fact that in practice India is still tied to its traditional discrimination. Such a cultural lag is probably inevitable, but this feeling only shows our impatience and does not take into account the reality of the situation, the centuries for which the individual has been neglected. In fact, nobody can foresee or foretell how long it will take India to become factually and in social practice completely democratic, giving every individual perfect equality and opportunity to make himself into whatever kind of individual he wants to be under the law. But the writing on the walls of time can be easily read. The modern Indian democratic ideal in society is no gift obtained from Western people alone, whose own ideas of democracy and freedom and universal individuality are quite new. India's contact with the West is certainly one of the main causes of the acceleration of the speed of reform. But the reforms are in the spirit and tradition of Indian society itself.

It is only now, quite late in her long history, that India has come to have an idea of the whole Indian community as such, the nationhood of the Indian people, secular and humanitarian and, as such, divorced from religion, and has come to think of the status of the individual and the whole community in a secular fashion. Today, even the poor, the illiterate, and the low-caste have all become conscious of their human rights, as well as their duties. So, now at long last, the original Indian spirit of the dignity and freedom of the individual shows signs of significant revival.

Question: Do we have enough historical factual data to justify the explanations you have given?

Answer: I do not know how to answer the question for the simple reason that it does not indicate any specific instance of factual or historical inaccuracy in the paper. After all, everything said in the paper has been supported by quotations from either authoritative texts or authoritative historians. Of course, quantitatively, many more references in support of all that I have said or maintained could have been given, but there was neither space nor time for such elaboration. I feel that the information in the paper is quite adequate under the circumstances.

Question: The Buddha was critical of the caste system, therefore did it not exist essentially in its later objectionable form prior to the Middle Ages?

Answer: This may be true, but the question does not challenge the statement made in the paper that the Vedic and earlier periods in Indian history were much more liberal and individualistic than the later degeneration in the medieval period, in which caste distinctions came to be based entirely on birth rather than on qualifications or profession. Distinctions of some kinds are bound to exist in all societies and at all times, and the Buddha, looking at the society of his time, must have criticized all distinctions from an exclusively moral standpoint. My point was and is simply that caste distinctions as they existed in the medieval period, or even in the British period, never existed in earlier India, a statement for which numerous references have already been given from the *Gītā,* the Epics, and even the Purāṇas and the Dharma-śāstras.

Question: Do you not confuse the social philosophy and the religious philosophy of India—for example, do not the Dharmaśāstras essentially ignore the spiritual goal of man, whereas you relate it intimately to social philosophy?

Answer: Such terms as *"mokṣa," "mukti,"* and *"niḥśreyas-siddhi"* (the attainment of the highest) are to be found in almost all basic texts. And, although it would be correct to say that the social goals in India had nothing to do with the individual's spiritual goal, almost all individuals in India are conscious of the idea of their own *mokṣa,* at least in the later stages of lives. The religious goal of life had a primacy even in the secular spheres of life. The separation of life into autonomous compartments of the political, legal, economic, and social spheres is a purely contemporary phenomenon in India.

Question: Your justification of duties as prior to the rights of the individual seem to be open to question. Would you elaborate a bit?

Answer: The point is simple enough. A society in which all individuals are conscious only of their individual rights and do their duties exclusively for fear of losing their rights would not be a strictly ethical society, nor would the behavior of the individual be strictly ethical. We can still imagine a society wherein all individuals are prompted and motivated in action solely by regard for their ethical duties in all circumstances. The Indians thus based their social structure on duties and obligations rather than on rights. The social end in both cases may be the same, but the difference lies in the Indian emphasis on the ethical motivation.

NOTES

1. What has been said here pertains primarily to Hindu society. The Buddhist in India, from the time of the Buddha himself, protested against all kind of class or birth distinction and gave full dignity and status to all individuals, but, later, Buddhism almost disappeared from the country of its origin. When the Muslims came to India in about the twelfth century A.D., though they adopted in practice the Hindu social evils of caste hierarchies in daily life, they were by their religion not supposed to have any social distinction between man and man. Thus, what pertains socially to Hindu society is true of the entire Indian social structure, in thought and practice.
2. J.L. Davies, *A Short History of Women* (New York: Viking Press, 1927), p. 172. Quoted in A. S. Altekar, *The Position of Women in Hindu Society* (Benares: The Cultural Publishing House, 1938), p. 407.

3. J. W. McCrindle, *Ancient India as Described by Megasthenes and Arrian* (Calcutta: Thacker, Spink & Co., 1877), p. 71. Quoted in P. V. Kane, *History of Dharmaśāstras,* 4 vols. (Poona: Bhandarkar Oriental Research Institute, 1941), Vol. II, Pt. 1, p. 183.
4. *Manu-smṛti,* X. 4.
5. *Bhagavad-gītā,* IX. 13.
6. *Bhāgavata-purāṇa,* VII. 9-10.
7. *Ibid.,* VII. 11-35.
8. *Ibid.,* VII. 23-32.
9. The *Rāmāyaṇa,* Āraṇyaka-kāṇḍa, 31-33.
10. *Chāndogya Upaniṣad,* IV. iv. 1-5. Jābāla went to learn *Brahma-vidyā* (knowledge of *Brahman)* from a *guru* who asked him the name of his father. He said he did not know but would ask his mother. His mother told him that she herself did not know because in her youth she slept with many young men. He told this to the *ṛṣi,* whereupon the latter said that he was fully entitled to the highest wisdom because few men and women dare tell the full truth.
11. Dakṣa, *Dakṣa-śāstra,* III. 22: *"Yathaivātmā 'parastadvad draṣṭavya sukhamicchatā sukhdukhāni tulyāni, yathātmani tathā pare."* Quoted in Kane, *op. cit.,* pp. 5n, 7n.
12. Devala: *"Ātmanah pratikūlāni pareśām na samācharet."* Quoted in Kane, *op. cit.,* p. 7n.
13. Mitāksara on *Yajur-veda,* I. 1.
14. *Mahābhārata,* I. 115. 36: *"Tyajet ekam Kulasyārthe, Kulam tyajet grāmam janapadāsyārthe, Ātmārthe prithīvim tyajet."*
15. *Mahābhārata,* I. 122. 44.
16. Abbé Dubois, *Hindu Manners, Customs and Ceremonies* (Oxford: Clarendon Press, 1877), p. 340.
17. Mahābhārata: *"Sarve ca sukhinah santu, sarve santu nirāmayah sarve bhadrāṇi paśyantu mā kaścit dukhabhāg bhavet."* Quoted in S. Radhakrishnan, *Religion and Society* (London: George Allen & Unwin Ltd., 1947), p. 91n.
18. Āpastamba, *Dharma-Sūtra,* I. vii. 2: "Āpastamba declares that there is nothing higher than the possession of the soul." Quoted in S. Radhakrishnan, *Religion and Society,* p. 62.
19. *Manu-smṛti,* X. 63: *"Ahiṁsā satyam asteyam, sauchamindriya nigrahaetam sāmāsikam dharmamcāturvaiṇeya abravin manuḥ."* Also, *Mahābhārata,* Śānti-parva, 72. 8-12.
20. Aśoka, 9th Edict Rock, in the *Corpus Inscriptionum Indicarum,* Vol. I.
21. Kauṭilya, *Artha-śāstra,* III. 13.
22. *Manu-smṛti,* VIII. 415, and Kane, *op. cit.,* pp. 183-185.
23. Sir John Malcolm, *Memoir of Central India* (London: Kingsbury, Parbury, & Allen, 1923), Vol. II, p. 202.
24. *Manu-smṛti,* IV. 176. Also, *Mahābhārata,* Śānti-parva, 160-161.
25. Kālidāsa, *Mālvikāgnimitram,* I. 2.
26. *Manu-smṛti,* VI. 89-90; III. 77-78.

Professor Zaehner and the Comparison of Religions

For about two hundred years now Indian philosophies and religions have been so persistently misrepresented and distorted by foreign writers that the Indians, both Hindus and Buddhists, are not only repelled by it all but have almost given up being concerned about it. It is indeed fortunate that there are still a few sound foreign interpreters of Indian thought and that the intelligent reader has begun to be discriminating about his choice of authors on Indian philosophies and religions. The number of accurate writers is increasing in contemporary times, and it is hoped that writers of the other category will soon disappear. But, amazingly enough, an extreme representative of the latter now speaks from the distinguished chair of the Spalding Professor of Eastern Religions and Ethics, University of Oxford, England. Because of his high position, the danger is great that he is more likely to mislead readers than are other non-Indian writers. There is some need, therefore, to correct, if possible, Zaehner himself, or if that is not possible, at least warn his readers against his "comparison of religions."

Zaehner had written a good book, *Mysticism, Sacred and Profane*. This was the reason I picked up a paperback edition of his *The Comparison of Religions,*[1] which appears to me to be the most astounding book in recent times on the subject. In this book Zaehner has perpetuated not only the most astonishing, if not shocking, misrepresentations about Hinduism and Buddhism as religions, but has scrapped as mere rubbish the noblest efforts of the best minds in India for over three thousand years in the realm of penetration into the mysteries, values, and destiny of human existence in preference to the exclusive Christian revelations which he mistakenly considers to be a rational examination of all the big religions of the world. I feel it, therefore, obligatory to deal with this book—but only insofar as it concerns Hinduism, for to do more than this would indeed involve writing a book longer than that written by Zaehner himself.

To start, it may be worthwhile to recall a few common distortions of Indian philosophical and religious thought presented by foreign writers over the years. By now, I suppose, they are all well known. Almost all of them have propagated the idea that both Indian philosophies and religions are immanentist, absolutist, or mystic; that the Hindus have no theism, no personal God, no two-way traffic between man and God; that the Hindus are interested only in the internal state of peace of mind, a characterless existence, are life-negating and pessimistic in their outlook, recognize no final reality, significance of ethical values, or moral obligation, believe in no independent authority of reason either in their philosophies or their religions, and show lack of interest in the problem of evil, etc. These are but a few of the prevalent, incorrect characterizations of Indian thought. There are a host of others, because Indians are supposed to be dominated also by numerous positive dogmas such as the law of *karma,* reincarnation, the law of *dharma,* desirelessness and non-attachment, *mokṣa,* absolute non-injury to any life, etc. The purpose of this article is neither to make a comprehensive list of such distortions nor to dispute them. If Zaehner, or anyone else, had said that Indian philosophical and religious literature includes all this but also much more which is different from this and which is no less representative and typical than the former, we would have had no quarrel with him. By temperament, Indians are too prone to find everything everywhere and will rest the matter there. But when a Spalding Professor of Eastern Religions and Ethics attempts to perpetuate the most unimaginable absurdities about Eastern religions, he must be corrected, even though it may be difficult to argue with a person who is sure that God reveals truth only to His chosen people and withholds it from all others.

There is nothing wrong in misreading the history of any philosophical literature—Indian, Chinese, Japanese, or Western—and forming one's own comparisons and contrasts on the basis of such misunderstandings, because one still remains at the standpoint or on the level of philosophy and can there be challenged on his own ground. It is more serious when someone compares and condemns, say, the philosophy of the Western world from the standpoint of Christian theology or religion, or judges the empirical religions of the world, not from any well-established logical standpoint applicable to all the religions of the world, but only from the standpoint and standard of a particular exclusive revelation. It is still worse if someone compares and condemns Indian philosophical and religious literature from the standpoint of Christian revelation alone, something to be ruled out at the very beginning. And yet, this is exactly what Zaehner has done in this book.

Let us have a look at the book. It contains five chapters: 1. Comparative Religion; 2 and 3. The Indian Contribution; 4. Prophets Outside Israel; 5. Consumatum Est; and an Appendix on the *Qur'ān* and the Christ.

From the beginning to the end, the book is full of fallacious and palpably absurd statements about Indian religions. It would require a much longer article to contradict him completely—or even adequately. Let me therefore confine myself within the space and will at my disposal, to the minimum of Hinduism alone, without paying any attention to what he says about Christianity, Buddhism, Islam, Zoroastrianism, and other religions. As will be seen from the Table of Contents, two of the five chapters which have been examined very carefully for this review deal with the Indian religions, Hinduism and Buddhism.

The author says that after lecturing on Christianity he took this opportunity "for coming to grips with the problem of how a Christian should regard the non-Christian religions . . . and to show how the main trends in Hinduism and Buddhism . . . meet and complete each other in the Christian revelation" (p. ix). He then sets the main theme of the book in showing that the "immanentist religions of India . . . do not contradict any essential Christian doctrine, and that their representations of incarnate God, incomplete though they are, are valid prefigurations of the God incarnate in Christ" (p. ix). Later, he states "Unless I am greatly mistaken, all the strands we have been trying to bring together in the different religions, meet *only* in *one* place, and that is the religion of Jesus Christ. In the person of Christ the two contradictions meet and are reconciled" (p. 180).[2] He ends: "My thesis is this, that Jesus Christ fulfills not only the law and the prophets of Israel but also the Prophet of Iran and the sages of India" (p. 184).

Zaehner is most welcome to all the merits of Christianity and all that the religion of Jesus Christ accomplishes. There is no quarrel with him on that. In fact, a Hindu should be the first to acknowledge the good that there is, not only in Christianity, but in all the religions of the world. Trouble starts when he misbrands Hinduism as an "immanentist" religion, or when he says that Hinduism and Buddhism "meet and complete each other in the Christian revelation," or that they "do not contradict any essential Christian doctrine," or that the Hindu incarnations of God "are valid prefigurations of the God incarnate in Christ," or that "all religions meet in only one place, and this the religion of Jesus Christ." This is not all. Later in the book he makes more astounding declarations about the Hindu ideas of God, revelation, and religion itself. It is a matter of some satisfaction that Zaehner has been careful to preface his conclusions with "Unless I am greatly mistaken" (p. 180). The purpose of this review is to tell him that he is most certainly and greatly mistaken, and that there is no doubt about that.

Zaehner's understanding of the Indian philosophies and religions of Hinduism and Buddhism is in a few respects remarkably correct. He often shows great insight into their true meanings. What is surprising from one point of view and shocking from another is that, in spite of his great learning, he has not been able to save himself from drawing absurd conclusions even from his correct premises. What could be the reasons for this? The main reason is that he first tries to look at Hinduism from an empirical and historical point of view but ends up by drawing his conclusions about it from the unempirical and revelatory standpoint of Christianity. This is his first great mistake. Another is that he has confused and identified Indian philosophical literature with Indian religion itself, which is unpardonable with regard to any people. He seems to be quite familiar with the philosophical literature of India—the portions that are translated into English—from the Vedas down to the Six Systems. Apparently, the only other book known to him is the *Bhagavad Gītā.* Besides these, he shows no signs, in his book, of being familiar with any other religious or devotional texts of India. This is not altogether his fault. Most foreigners are familiar only with the above texts, but they have not drawn Zaehner's conclusion that there is no real theism in India and other such absurd views about Hinduism. If he had read the *Purāṇas,* the two important epics, the whole mass of the theistic and devotional literature of the Hindus, the lives of India's hundreds of saints and devotees, and if he had observed without prejudice the daily life and worship of millions of Hindus through the centuries, he could have never come to the conclusion that Hinduism had no God or theism. It passes one's comprehension how anyone could possibly come to that astounding conclusion unless one believes that humanity was bereft of God until He revealed himself to man in the person of Christ. In other words, he has first identified the philosophical literature of the Hindus with their religious literature and, what is worse, has applied his revelatory Christian standards for judging them both. In fact, he has a fixed and fanatic standard for what it means to be religious or to have God, and then judges whatever he finds in Hinduism from that exclusive standpoint.

This is not all. He carried his prejudices further into the realm of Indian philosophy itself. "In India, except in the purely popular cults, religion is never divorced from philosophy" (p. 167). One would like to know what ideas he has of philosophy, and what philosophy the forty million illiterates in India could have had for centuries to divorce it from their religion? In the strict sense, neither philosophy nor religion could ever be involved with each other except accidentally. Still, even if a religion were to be essentially involved with philosophy as Zaehner charges Hinduism to be, it is far better that it be so than that it be involved with revelation as Zaehner wrongly wants it to be.

As an instance of religion being involved with philosophy, Zaehner says that "no religion can wholly satisfy which is based fundamentally on the total rejection of the phenomenal world either as an illusion or as a prison in which the immortal spirit is held helplessly captive" (p. 168). Quite a few observations can be made on the above. First, it is absolutely wrong to say that Hindu philosophy or religion recommends a total rejection of the phenomenal world either as an illusion or as a prison in which the immortal is helplessly held! What both philosophy and religion recommend in India is the non-finality of the changing world as we perceive and experience it. The progress to transcendence in both Hindu philosophy and religion is through the fulfillment of the phenomenality of the world itself. There is not, nor can there be, any skipping over the phenomenal world. Secondly, the illusoriness of the world or its rejection as a philosophy is, after all, held by only one school of philosophy. It may be wrong, and its opposite, namely, the final or absolute reality of the phenomenal world may be the correct school of philosophy. But for Zaehner both should be irrelevant, because religion is not to be involved with philosophy at all, either right or wrong.

But more importantly, in Hinduism the immortal spirit is not at all held helplessly captive, because the entire purpose of Hinduism as a religion is the *release* of man from captivity, i.e., the "hopefulness" of the escape from captivity. Zaehner conveniently forgets that, speaking of God in the Upaniṣads, he himself contradicts this earlier statement when he says "Why does God imprison man in matter, only to *release* him at his appointed time?" (p. 115).[3] How is the above consistent with the immortal spirit in Hinduism being held "helplessly captive"? This is how Zaehner by the injection of a single word, "helplessly," distorts the whole philosophy and religion of Hinduism and quite gratuitously blames writers like Aurobindo, Hiriyanna, and Radhakrishnan for being inspired by Christian influence for propagating the view that the world is not an illusion, for surely Hinduism is much older than any one or all of them.

Zaehner sees in Indian philosophy—except in Rāmānuja—only the absorption of man into the Absolutistic Brahman. One wonders how anybody could see nothing but monism in the varied schools of Indian philosophy, when everybody should know that Absolute Monism is only one school out of six notably non-monist but equally, it not more, important schools of Hindu philosophy. That Zaehner had no access to the religiously theistic literature of the Hindus is not altogether his fault, but such sweeping characterizations about the entire philosophical literature as being monistic cannot be justified even after a misreading of the history of Indian philosophy itself. It is difficult to understand how anyone could possibly identify Indian philosophies with Advaita Vedānta, Yoga, or Jainism alone when in every age there have been equally, if not more pervasive philosophical systems constantly opposing it. Advaita Vedānta without its important opponents has never even been mentioned in the philosophical literature of India. Even in the twentieth century, during which time the monistic misrepresentation of India has been so widespread outside India, Advaita Vedānta has had the most uncompromising opponent in the person of Swami Dayananda Śarasvati, who is regarded by his followers as great a philosopher as Sankara himself and who fought all his life most brilliantly against the Absolute Vedāntins throughout the length and breadth of India. This is the philosophical history of India in our own lifetime. Of course, even immediately after Sankara, a whole wave of qualified monisms, dualisms, and pluralisms overwhelmed Absolutism, as it were. One wonders why the factual and objective history in the realms of pure thought and literature of a nation should be as misread as its political history. There may be some justification in misreading political histories of different nations because emotions are difficult to divorce from politics, but there is no reason why this should be done in the realm of the philosophy or the religion of a people. But, of course, as someone has said, religion, too, is after all nothing more than the noblest emotion of man which occasionally can be the worst obsession of a few.

Zaehner has truly emphasized the fact that the Indian religions are empirical, i.e., that they are "man's unaided attempt to come to terms with the divine which cannot therefore be treated as being a revelation" (p. ix). He is to be congratulated on this real point of a fundamental contrast between Hinduism, on the one hand, and the revealed religions of the world, on the other. One wonders why he has not adhered to this distinction in his comparisons between Hinduism and Christianity and why for the purpose of this book he has treated Hinduism as being on a par with the revelatory religion of Christianity. Let us examine his reason for this.

His reason is that these religions (Hinduism and Buddhism) claim to be "revelations." "There is no doubt that the Hindus regard their own Veda as being in *some sense* a revelation" (p. ix). It is exactly here that Zaehner has erred grossly. The Hindus do regard their Vedas in *some sense* as a revelation, and they do regard their Rāma and Krishna as divine incarnations, but only in *some sense*, as Zaehner himself has said, and not at all in the exclusive sense in which a Christian or a Zaehner would like to regard them. The meaning of the term revelation when a Hindu uses it and when a Christian uses it is *totally different*. If Zaehner had maintained his original insight that Indian religions are not revelations but only unaided discoveries of the Hindus in the realm of the Divine, he would have easily seen that none of the conclusions he draws about them actually follow. Though Zaehner says that the Indian religions are not revelatory religions, he treats and judges them completely as if they were. In comparisons between religions, one can certainly draw such contrasts as empirical and revelatory, as Zaehner has done, but then, one certainly should hesitate to evaluate the one from the standpoint of the other.

It is true that the term "revealed" is used by the Hindus for the Vedas, and the idea of divine incarnation is used for Rāma, Krishna, Vishnu, and other earlier deities, but not at all in the sense in which a Christian regards Jesus Christ as the Son of God, or the Gospels as his revelations. The term "revelation," too, is empirical in the Hindu mind. When the content of a book or the character of a hero is considered as revealed, it means only that they are regarded as truer than others, and it merely shows that the highest regard and respect is given them in the minds of their followers. That the Vedas are revealed means only that they are so old as to be timeless, and the knowledge therein is supposed to have been directly or intuitively known to their authors and not that God actually spoke to them. That Rāma and Krishna are held to be divine incarnations means that they were such great men in their times, that their characters and personalities showed such values that they have become idolized and have become the ideals for men for all ages. Incarnation of godhood is a Hindu's highest term of praise for men or things. The Hindus will not be surprised at all if Gandhi in the distant future comes to be regarded as an "Avatāra" or a divine incarnation by millions of people in India. That is why the Hindus find no difficulty in accepting the Buddha, Christ, or Muhammad, or anyone else as divine incarnations. Zaehner knows this, too, for he says "Krishna, in any case is no prophet in the old testament sense.... Rather, perhaps, we should say he is the idea of God made incarnate in the Indian mind" (p. 135). They are not *the exclusive and the only incarnation* of God in the sense in which Jesus is regarded by orthodox Christians. Also, the Hindus can laugh at their revealed books and divine incarnations, and criticisms of them are not uncommon on the part of their followers. All this could not have been unknown to Zaehner. His statement, therefore, that Hinduism as an unaided attempt to come to terms with the Divine seems to be singularly barren can be true only when one agrees with him that nothing but exclusive revelation as believed in by the orthodox Christians or Muslims can alone be fertile.

Zaehner loses all his points in this book if the Hindus do not claim (as they in fact do not) that their religion is a revealed one. In fact, it could not have been hidden from Zaehner that Hinduism is not the name given to the religion by the Hindus themselves and that the name for their religion in earlier times was Ārya Dharma, or the religion of the Āryas, and, in later times, Sanātana Dharma, or the eternal religion. This is so, not because their religion was once and for all revealed for them but because the principles underlying it were discovered over centuries as truths for all empirical seekers. The Hindus discovered the mysteries of religious life exactly as we today empirically discover the mysteries of the physical universe. To the Hindus there is no revealed religion, exactly as there is no revealed physics or geography. When the Hindus pray to Rāma and Krishna, they pray only to God in that name which can without loss of religious value be replaced by any other name, say that of Christ. The only way to look at Hinduism and Buddhism is to find out what they have discovered to be the nature of man and the universe or what has been their attitude of prayer and worship towards the highest power in the cosmos. Looking at the Hindus and the Buddhists from the point of view of a dogmatic and an exclusive revelatory attitude is altogether irrelevant. Zaehner also knows that Hinduism encourages all religions to follow their own prayers and worship. But, this, as Zaehner says, "is to the prophet always unthinkable, for it compromises the truth and... what they worship is evil." Also, "Religions are not, as for Krishna, approximations to the Truth. They are either true (his own) or false (all others). There can be no compromise" (p. 138). Hinduism can never agree to this. It is too rational for that. Until "the Truth" is known (and who but Zaehner can say that it *is* known), all religions will have to be content with approximations to the truth.

Zaehner accepts the Hindu scriptures when they say that "it is not enough to know only that (God) exists but we must know His nature and His will." But he asks, "And how can one know His nature and His will except by prophetic revelation" (p. 183), and, if only by prophetic revelation, then, of course, only by Christian revelation. It is therefore proved to him that Hinduism is not a religion in the true sense of the term. When Zaehner, a theist, argues against an atheist, it is understandable, but his arguments become completely distorted when he attempts to declare that no theist is a theist unless he is a Christian theist. In *The Comparison of Religions,* far from succeeding in pointing out the deficiencies of non-Christian religions, Zaehner has failed to present even a moderately acceptable picture of Christianity.

Zaehner says that the "immanentist" religions of India do not contradict any essential Christian doctrine and that their "representations of an incarnate God, incomplete though they are, are valid prefigurations of God incarnate in Christ" (p. ix). It is wrong, in the first place, to say that the religions of India (and the same is true of the philosophies of India) are "immanentist." That they do not contradict any essential Christian doctrine may be left without comment (though open to doubt). I wonder if Zaehner has noticed the contradiction in his two statements which he made in the same breath. How can any religion be only immanentist and not contradict any essential Christian doctrine? The second part of his statement is completely wrong. The representation of an incarnate God in Hinduism is as complete in every respect as man's imagination can make it, unless we assume at the start that the incarnation of God in Christ alone is complete and final. Zaehner could not have been unaware of the fact that the Hindus have at least ten prefigurations of the incarnate God in different forms of life and that such a great atheist as the Buddha was the last one added to these prefigurations of God. To compare the Hindu empirical prefigurations of God with the Being of Christ is to compare two altogether different outlooks of mind. That the Hindu incarnations of God are prefigurations of Christ, valid or invalid, is only historically true in as much as they were made by man much before Christ. There is nothing identical between the two as incarnations of God, because they are not supposed to be revelatory in the sense in which Christ is taken to be.

Zaehner's next comment is that "whereas the Christian starts with the idea of God, the Hindus and the Buddhists do not" (p. 16). This is so obvious and true that no non-revelationist can ever find any fault with it, for either God revealed himself to man before Christ or he did not. If he did reveal himself to man, Zaehner's statement is false, and if he did not reveal himself before Christ, the statement is obviously true. But if God did not reveal himself before Christ, the fault lies with God and not with man. I do not see how anyone can find fault with man for not "beginning with God." It is a great tribute to the Hindus that they actually found and discovered God independently of Christ. Rather than give the Hindus some credit for the discovery of God, Zaehner's study of Hinduism, on the contrary, has taught him that the Hindus are a Godless people and that they care only for a state of timeless and eternally peaceful existence in which "you will have passed beyond pleasure and pain into a perfect peace where you will no longer even feel the need-for God" (p. 19). This is another instance of Zaehner's confusing identification of the non-theistic schools of the philosophy of Sāṅkya-Yoga, Jainism, and the Advaita Vedānta with the entire body of philosophical and religious schools and at the expense of Indian theism and religion in general.

It is certainly surprising, if not shocking, to think that hardly anyone—anyone much less acquainted with Hinduism than Zaehner must be—has thought of Hinduism in these terms. In fact, until now, the world has associated Hinduism only with its Godliness and its preoccupation with a divine life, and it is this aspect of Indian life that has been assumed to be responsible for India's material backwardness. But now we are told, here, that the Hindus not only do not have a God but that they do not even *need* one. This only shows that even the best of scholarship can play mischief if the mind or the intellect behind it is not free from prejudices or orthodoxy. Any orthodoxy can turn truth into untruth. The whole history of Hinduism is against Zaehner, for in India those who have not felt the need of God have at least never hidden their feelings but have openly proclaimed them in profound and serious arguments. God has never been smuggled into Hinduism through any back door (revelation included). God in India has survived for centuries the onslaught of the materialists, the Buddhists, the Jains, and the Mīmāṃsakas. But, of course, if God stands for someone revealed through a particular chosen son of man at a particular time and place, then it is not possible at all for anyone excepting those chosen people to have a God. The Hindus and other non-Christians should not be blamed for this. According to Zaehner, the great weakness of the Indians is that with them "The question of the existence and nature of God is, when all is said and done, of secondary importance" (p. 43). "Basically they are not interested in what we would call 'God' at all" or still, "they do not teach you very much about God, but they do teach you a great deal about the immortality of the soul and the Absolute (p. 57). His reason for making such a palpably false statement is that he finds the hitherto Indian philosophical literature published in English full of phrases like the Yogic Samādhi, Jain Arhathood, Advaitic absorbtion into Brahman, self-realization, etc. It has already been pointed out that, since non-theistic trends have existed in India alongside the theistic ones, it does not follow that God does not exist in India or that he is of secondary importance. In the West, too, many forms of agnostic or atheistic schools of philosophy thrive, but no one draws the conclusion that there is therefore no God in Christianity.

His great complaint against Hinduism is that in it we do not find "anything at all comparable to the old testament idea of an intensely personal God operating in and through His people in history. The old testament is revelation in the strictest sense; God progressively reveals His purpose to His chosen people, and there is always a looking forward to the coming of the Kingdom of God at the end of time, when Israel will be restored to its rightful greatness" (p. 69). The Hindus are glad that they cannot subscribe to any such totally unacceptable revelation of religion.

One of Zaehner's new ways of distorting Hinduism is that he sets Buddhism against Hinduism on the score of the Buddha's non-admittance of the existence of the Absolute of the Upaniṣads of the Hindus. While this certainly is a point of opposition between the Buddhistic philosophy and the Absolutism of the Upaniṣads prevalent in the Buddha's time, it has never been a point of opposition between Hinduism and Buddhism as religions. In Indian philosophical and religious literature, Buddhism has always been called an atheistic school whose meaning certainly cannot be only unbelief in the Absolute. In India, the Buddhists have always been called atheists and not non-absolutists. Why should Zaehner not emphasize the atheism of the Buddha against the theism of the Hindus rather than make capital of the differences between them only on the problem of the doctrine of momentariness versus the principle of permanence passes comprehension? To continue, "Hinduism and Buddhism, on the other hand, are not vitally interested in the problem of evil" (p. 150). How Christianity is more vitally interested in the problem than are other religions is not made clear to the non-Christian. It is interesting to note that a few pages later he says, "Nor should we be shocked by the fact that Islam was spread by the sword" (p. 161). This makes one suspect at least of the author's idea of Christianity's interest in the problem of evil. Again, "Christian Ethics is not what makes Christianity unique" (p. 181), sounds rather unusual to a Hindu who has always regarded the ethical commandments of Christianity much more highly than the dogma of the virgin birth, the scandal of the cross, the resurrection of the body, etc.

Again, "In the West we hold that man is a creature and his right attitude to God is one of creatureliness; and creatureliness expresses itself in worship and sacrifice. Neither the Vedānta nor Buddhism accepts this" (p. 103). So far as man's being a creature is concerned, I thought the entire Hindu population not only accepts it but lives it too. One wonders, however, why Vedāntist and the Buddhist should "accept it" at all. It is not for them to accept it, that is only for the non-absolutist Hindus to do. In fact, the Hindus of India by and large think of the Vedāntist and the Buddhist and the Jains alone as opponents of God with whom they have no truck on that score. I again wonder why one compares the religious attitude of either the West or the East with the absolutists, the agnostics, the mystics, or the atheists of these countries.

It is a natural shift from Zaehner's identification of atheistic monism with theistic Hinduism to his account of the achievement of "total *vairāgya*, or stilling of the affections, whether they be for good or evil" (p. 21), as one of the important religious doctrines of the Indians. This is a point on which enough has already been written and yet misunderstandings have not yet been cleared up. Suffice it to say that the stilling of passions, mostly ignoble and those that are obstacles to the attainment of spiritual ends, has always been a common doctrine of moral preparation towards spiritual goals on the part of Hinduism *as well as Christianity.* Also, no Hindu theist or God-intoxicated devotee has ever wanted to get rid of his passion for God. The lives of the millions of religious Hindus are ample testimony to it long before Hinduism came into contact with Christianity. Leaving Hinduism aside, why are such teachings as the following from even the Buddha himself not attended to by scholars? In his sermon to Sadhu Sinha, the Buddha says: "It is true, Sinha, that I denounce activities, but only activities that lead to evil in words, thought, and deeds. It is true, Sinha, that I preach extinction, but only the extinction of pride, lust, evil thought, and ignorance, not that of forgiveness, charity, and truth." Many similar passages can be cited from Hinduism—and from medieval Christian saints also. But those who do not believe in theism as the highest state of man's existence and, on the contrary, believe in an eternal, experienceless state of existence, are certainly entitled to advocate man's rising above all passions, both good and evil, because they have a different philosophy or ideal of life than that of communion with God. The suppression of passions is not unknown to Christianity either.

The important question is whether Zaehner is comparing Christianity with Hinduism as a religion or with agnostic and atheistic schools of thought in India. If the former, all his conclusions are wrong, and, if the latter, why? In many of his charges against Hinduism, Zaehner forgets that they are equally true of Christianity also. For instance, such teachings as that of "two worlds," and of the separation of the "eternal from the perishable," etc., are by no means exclusive to Hinduism.

The Hindu doctrine of the transmigration of souls is also not as Zaehner understands it. The transmigration of souls follows logically from the undying characteristic of the soul itself which cannot be disembodied unless the soul achieves its set task of the highest ideal of life. A man cannot be denied his apparatus of body and mind through which alone he can accomplish those desires and ambitions of perfection which cannot be achieved in one single span of life. This is not to defend or minimize the difficulties that there are in this or any alternate religious doctrine. The point here is simply to have them properly understood as propounded by their authors.

What, according to Zaehner, is the greatest weakness of Hinduism is perhaps its greatest strength, namely, its lack of revelation.[4] In fact, it is so difficult to understand why he calls it a weakness when he himself has once accepted Hinduism as a non-revelatory religion. Is it because a particular kind of historical revelation is all that is meant be revelation? After all, there can be only three situations with regard to revelation and Hinduism: (1) that Hinduism is not revelatory in which case you cannot judge it by any revelatory standards; (2) that Hindus, too, claim to be revelationists but have an altogether different meaning of revelation, in as much as any perception of eternal truth anywhere by any persons may be called revelation; (3) that Hindus believe in revelation in the same exclusive sense in which the Christians do, and therefore their religion, too, should be judged by the Christian standards of revelation. Actually, the first and second positions alone are applicable to Hinduism, and it is absurd to look at Hinduism from the third standpoint. Even with regard to the last interpretation, Zaehner should see that, if as he maintains, "in the Christian west, on the other hand, religion has been primarily concerned with what is deemed to be divine revelation and *with the correct interpretation of the content* of that revelation" (p. 56),[5] then the fact that the divine revelation needs a correct interpretation takes away much of its character as a revelation. If, according to the revelationists, it is the interpretation which is going to decide the contents of revelation, then the revelationist has given up his case altogether. According to Zaehner, "Experience, when divorced from revelation, often leads to absurd and wholly irrational excesses" (p. 57). Has it occurred to him that revelation, when divorced from experience, not only often leads, but has many times in history actually led to absurd and even more irrational excesses?

To summarize, the whole argument of the book runs something like this: the Indians, the Hindus and the Buddhists both, have made great contributions in the realm of the highest psychological stages to which man can attain and have made great and praiseworthy suggestions about the nature of the universe and its relation to man, but they do not have or believe in the revelation of Jesus Christ, hence they do not and cannot teach much about God. This kind of argument does not need any comment. If, however, Zaehner is obsessed by the idealistic absolutism of the Upaniṣads and the Vedānta, let him remember that in India these have the same relationship with Hinduism as Christianity has with Hegelianism or dialectical materialism. There is no limit to Zaehner's absurdities about Indian religions. "Indian theology, then, starts as Dialectical Materialism, and proceeds progressively from materialism to Idealism" (p. 64). It is difficult to imagine such a characterization of Indian theology until one reads Zaehner. If theology is to be understood in the usual sense, how possibly can dialectical materialism ever be characterized as theology? Upaniṣadic "Brahman is food," "Brahman is air," and so forth were, according to Zaehner, laid down as principles of dialectical materialism "millenia before Marx and Engels were ever heard of" (p. 63). This is just one more example of Zaehner's continuous misuse of terms and the lack of any serious distinction between generalized thought and theology on the one hand, and religion and philosophy on the other.

His two observations about the *Bhagavad Gītā* would not be amiss here. Zaehner says "this is perhaps the greatest weakness of the theology of the Bhagavad Gītā. God has no purpose in creating the world" (p. 129). It is as if he or any other book of religion had actually found the answer to the purpose of God's having created the world. One would have thought that the only answer any philosophy or philosophy of religion could possibly find was that no philosophy or religion has any answer to these ultimate questions. If one knows the answer before he even understands the question, as Zaehner seems to do, he only sound absurder than the absurd. One more of his quotations concerning the *Gītā* is worth giving here. "To sum up, Brahman in the *Gītā* is cosmologically primal matter *(prakṛti,* or Māyā); psychologically, it is the realization of immortality. The confusion is appalling" (p. 126). There may be many confusions in the *Gītā,* but this summing up of the entire text of the *Gītā* is more than appalling. Zaehner in great irony and praise of the *Bhagavad Gītā* says, "this is the highest Word, the 'most mysterious of all,' a thing unheard of in India before—God loves man" (p. 133). If this unheard-of-before message of God's loving man appears in the *Bhagavad Gītā* as Zaehner says, does he realize that the message was heard of much before Christ, or not much later than that, even if the latest dates are accepted for the *Mahābhārata.* Finally, "the *Gītā* offers the promise, not yet the fulfillment" (p. 179). This is obvious, because the fulfillment, for the author, had to come as if by a cosmic law only in the form of the New Testament.

To conclude, if the sole purpose of Zaehner's *The Comparison of Religions* was to prove, by a travesty of reasoning, that no religion in the world except orthodox and dogmatic Christianity is a religion at all or can possibly meet any religious need of man, Zaehner need not have taken the trouble to write two hundred pages to *prove* it.

NOTES

1. Robert C. Zaehner, *The Comparison of Religions* (Boston: Beacon Press, 1962). Page numbers in parentheses throughout this chapter refer to Zaehner, *The Comparison of Religions.*
2. Italics mine.
3. Italics mine.
4. See "Testimony in Indian Philosophy," this volume, chapter 3.
5. Italics mine.

A Comparison between the Eastern and Western Portraits of Man in Our Time

There is a level deep within man where there is no difference at all in humanity between a man from the East or the West, the North or the South. This is an elemental, natural, primary, and basic human level. The need for comfort, food, housing, satisfactions of the emotional needs of affection, a feeling of security, love, and sex are common to humanity as such. Affectionate regard from family and friends around, capacities for nobler and higher loyalties and devotion, and gratefulness are deep down common to the majority of all people regardless of their geographical differences. Human infants and children of all different races and geographically different locations are all alike. They are all just human infants, so is the love of the mothers for their infants. As a poet said, a man's a man for all that. Does man not laugh when you tickle him? Does he not bleed when you cut him? Is not one man hurt or pleased as another is?

There are, however, differences between men, but the point to be made is that these differences are adult-conditioned and artificial in the sense that they are the products of education, and political, economic, religious, social, and cultural training. They are adult-made and can be remolded and changed if man wanted to, that is to say, if man was prepared to rise above his present national, patriotic, and racial levels of existence regardless of his national likes, dislikes, and prejudices, he could realize the unity of man all around. What then are the differences, nurtured and educated between man and man? What are the differences today in the two portraits of man—the Eastern and the Western?

To begin with my portrait of a Western man, it must be remembered that I am an Indian, an Easterner, and also an individual with my own reflections. No claim, therefore, to absolute objectivity or truth is to be attributed to what are only my own impressions. I can classify my own reflections and experiences in some very broad points.

The Western man is certainly more dynamic in regard to both his own ambitions as well as his fight with the environment. I do not think I can attribute the same kind of dynamic urge to Easterners, with the possible exception of the Japanese. I am not taking into account the Communist world, perhaps, for the Easterner there has changed or is just changing in this regard. But, by and large, for Eastern man, I think this is correct. He has to this day produced the image of a comparatively easy-going individual with regard to both his surrounding as well as his own personality. He is easily contented. The causes are not taken into account here. They may be climatic or cultural. But the differences are there, and the image stays, barring of course the exceptions.

The above is also connected with our concept of the dignity of man. Men in different parts of the hemisphere understand the term "dignity of man" differently. The Easterner keeps a gradation in man in regard to the spiritual, the moral, the intellectual, and the physical; and only after these come the financial and the political man. The dignity of man is understood within the above gradations. It is not that he belittles the dignity of the manual worker or the merely rich, but that he still likes to keep the dignity of a man of letters, a moral hero, or above all a spiritual saint. The Westerner, in comparison, would emphasize the dignity of man just as man and would prefer to minimize or eliminate heirarchies. The idea of the dignity of man is compatible, say, in India, with the higher degree of dignity of an illiterate saint or a hero than it would be in the West, where it would perhaps be more easily conceded that a saint would be a better saint if he was literate. This is something which would not be conceded by an Easterner—at least not readily.

There is also a rather important distinction between man in the East and West which is worth noting. The idea of the dignity of man is related to the Western concept of the "rights" of man, and any man in the West, no matter what his position or education is always conscious of his rights, which no one dares infringe upon. In the East, the importance is not so much on a man's rights as on his "duties." As contrasted with the "rights-conscious" individual in the West, an Easterner is a "duty-conscious" individual. It is not that the Easterner loses his rights. Rights and duties are the two sides of the same coin. It is just the emphasis on the duties of the individual rather than his rights, which have been put before him for thousands of years, that even today determine his personality in a variety of relationships toward his family members, society, and the state. For a duty-performing individual, the rights are supposed to follow automatically.

Another point worth mentioning in connection with the portrait of man in the East and the West is the distinction between "being" and "having." In India, especially, and in other parts of the Eastern world, the concept of man being somebody in his own self is more important than having or not having a number of things. The concept of having or "possessing" applies only to objects and things externally related to man. Money, land, wealth, or jewelry, and other such items can alone be had or possessed. The moral or spiritual qualities of a man are not had or possessed in a similar way. They are an inner part of his own self. One does not possess or have musical, poetic, moral, or spiritual qualities in the same way as one possesses shirts. A man just *is* a poet, a singer, a hero, or a saint, and it is his "isness" through which he creates or expresses himself. One can possess a lot of poetic or spiritual treasures without being a music creator or a poet in his ownself, which is all that is important. One is speaking here mostly of Indian tradition. It would be rarer in the West to have an individual who is just what he is in himself without regard to any possessions whatever, even of what he has himself created. At least in the West, "Being in one's ownself" and "possessing" go together. But this is not necessarily so in my mind of the picture of man in India. To speak only of two well-known examples, Gandhi and Vinoba, would be to ignore the many other completely unknown men in India who prize only what they are in their own characters and personalities besides which they possess nothing. This is not to belittle worldly possessions, but only to point out a distinction that it is better to be than to have, and that being is higher than having. The distinction is perhaps only an attitude of living but whatever it is, it is perhaps more important to an Indian and most Easterners than to Westerners. It is the same with many great souls in the West, including Christ who said, "What would it profit man if he gained the world and lost his soul?" But this has not been reflected enough today in the picture of Western man. It refers to an inwardness in the life of an Eastern man rather than in a Western man whose life is lived more on an external than an internal plane. Externalization of life is more the Western mode of living than the Indian. Let me illustrate this point. An Indian will travel throughout the length and breadth of his country just to meet a saint, a real "sadhu," without ever raising a question in his mind as to who the saint is, what he does, or what his occupation is. What matters is that he is going to meet a saint. To be a saint in itself is completely satisfying to the Indian. Nothing more is to be known except that the man he will meet *is* a saint. I have often tried to explain this attitude to Westerners. First, they tell me that they do not travel only to meet a saint. And before they meet him, they would like to know who he is, what he does with himself, how he spends his time, and many other things which he must do besides being a saint, just as we are all men and also have occupations.

The learned man in the East has a prestige of his own which far exceeds the prestige which is bestowed to any other calling. It appears that a learned man in the West does not stand in the same position. To be simply known as learned is enough in the East to earn respect from all around. To be sure, in the West, too, the learned man is cared for, sought after, and honored, but in the world of today, he is also a victim of liberalization and leveling. The learned man has prestige, but only in the sense that he is well paid, in terms of money. The point is that one can pay a learned man much more today than he has ever been paid before, but that does not exhaust the meaning of genuine respect, which is due in society irrespective of his wealth or poverty.

Another image that I have of the Western man in this age of democracy, equality, and freedom is that of an undue leveling of all personal heirarchies in matters of mind and achievements. A certain kind of personal heirarchy between men and minds is good both for the individual and for man. This needs a little explanation. It occurs to me, and I may be all wrong in this, that the individuals in the West today do not have the same kind of personal adoration for a philosopher like Plato, Kant, or any other great thinker of the past as I have for them. Being in the same field, I find I keep myself at a distance from them and that I feel quite at the bottom while they are all at the top. This would be so even if I were the greatest philosopher of the twentieth century. I have a hierarchy in my mind with regard to their minds and achievements. I find this lacking in the West. I sometimes wonder if a sculptor or painter of any advanced Western country realizes in his own mind a sense of heirarchy with regard to Michelangelo, Leonardo da Vinci or Raphael. But I suspect that an individual who is a great Western sculptor or a painter might feel that he is equally great if not greater. He will perhaps feel that only his creations and tools and designs are different, and there is no difference in greatness. He might be equally great.

This leveling of the individuals to which I am referring above is perhaps due to the importance of the "public." It is the public that sets up standards in all spheres of our lives, and it is strange to say that a man in the West is more prone to live up to the public standards than is a man in the East.

Strange that in an age of freedom, we should be so afraid to be free from the public taste even in inconsequential matters. The need to conform, in so many inconsequential matters, is perhaps a trait of the Western individual, there are exceptions, of course. We are thinking here only of the larger majorities. A passion for his own individuality, and I am using the term "passion" in an earnest sense, is associated in my mind more with an Easterner than a Westerner. A Westerner is also an individual, but he is perhaps so only when he is alone or when he does not show any one of his individual traits in public. The desire to be like others is more ingrained in him. Examples need not be multiplied. A desire to conform to the public show rather than to conform to his own passionate idols for which his soul is craving is greater in the Western man. This can be pushed so far that, in most cases, it becomes a question of whether or not the individual in the West has any other craving of his own soul except to be a model of highest conformity to the abstract called the "Public" with a capital P. Peculiar, idiosyncratic, and crazy, are terms more commonly applied to individuals in the West than in the East.

This leveling up which is a weakness in the mind and soul of an individual is probably not the best thing for human and spiritual evolution and progress of the inner man. Some degree of a heirarchy of higher and lower personal achievements of mind and heart between individuals and and individual's own estimation was a good feeling in olden times, and it appears to be lost more speedily in the West than in the East. The individuals are quickly being leveled in the West, maybe without any fault on their part. Only something should be done to encourage the other kind of attitude, too, both in East and West.

Another picture that I have in my mind of the typical Western man in comparison with the Indian is, unless he is unusual and non-representative, is of his dread of being alone, by "alone" I mean when he is not fed by external stimuli of sound and sight from the external world. A good illustration of being just by one's self would be the situation of waiting. I have hardly, if ever, seen a Western man happy with himself alone, listening to the radio, watching television, or pursuing a journal or newspaper. If I have to wait an hour for a haircut, I could wait without any aid from contact with the external world. My mind will furnish me with all that I will need for my thinking and reflecting. This is not being introspective, but only refers to an inwardness and a lesser dependence on things and contacts supplied or given from the outside.

The mind can always furnish its own furniture from within itself. Not to be able to live without things being "given," I take as a kind of passivity of mind. At first, I had a great admiration for the Western man in this respect, for no matter in what situation or time I saw him, he was always occupied with listening to music, reading, talking, or doing something. I thought it was so good to be always doing something and not being lazy or wasting time. Later, it occurred to me that too much of that kind of activity produces a passivity and an inability of the mind to be independent and just by one's self. An internal activity of mind is its natural habitat and perhaps it is not desirable to lose it. I fancy, it would be a greater punishment to a Westerner than to an Easterner, or, specifically to an Indian, to be confined to his own solitariness without any kind of contact with the external world of books, human beings, animals, pictures or sounds. Solitariness has its own rewards, which when properly cultivated enriches and develops the human mind.

Another point I want to make is about the quality of obedience in men's characters and personalities. Obedience has today a derogatory quality in terms of civic and family life. It is perhaps reserved only for military life and training. This is a quality of the age in our times, and given time it may change in the East and in India also, but today the difference exists in some measure between men from the East and from the West. It is still, in most homes and societies in the East, considered good and desirable for younger boys and girls to cultivate and practice obedience toward their parents and elders, in life at home and outside. Ordinary courtesies are responded to in India by members of the family or an organization just because a father, mother, wife, brother, or an elder wants something and for no other reason. That some things be done just because they are wanted by a relative and for no other reason is losing its hold in the West. The family may find other reasons for obedience and obey the wishes of the elders, but will resent the mere quality of obedience being attributed to them. This change is coming in the Eastern world too, but still there is a difference in this respect. An Indian son, daughter, or wife will be proud of the fact that he or she is obedient to the elder for no reason other than obedience because of the relationship of age and blood. Children today will not pick up the evening paper or a glass of water and give it to the father if asked to do so when they are watching television or listening to the stereo. They would rather ask the father to get it himself, but I was raised differently, am still different, and would like to remain so. This form of obedience only adds to the charms and comforts of life and does not take away either the dignity of man or destroy one's freedom, equality, or independence.

The next point is the image in my mind of a Western man as an individual who is more a product of the substitution of nature and life than nature and life itself. The Western individual would prefer to improve upon his natural body. He does to a large extent succeed in what he calls the "improving upon his nature-given body." His manners, ways of talking and behaving, are also an imitation of what his advanced and honored society has given him. There is a tendency to check what are called in the Western world, the indecent, natural impulses, like sneezing, tooth-picking, and scratching one's body. One's diet, what one eats and drinks, is, by and large, a substitute of what is found in natural life. The meaning of words like "fresh" has changed. In the Western world, it no longer means freshly picked from plants or immediately slaughtered animals. Anything kept under scientific and hygenic conditions for mouths is also termed "fresh." The point is that the typical life in the Western world is more removed from the elemental, natural, and fresh world of nature and life. This applies to Western man's emotional and sexual life also. These are lived more under artificially produced conditions and life and satisfied, as it were, in a second-hand manner. The more artificial are things and life, the more Western they are. It is yet, thank heaven, not so in the East, where life is still in a more natural state with all its manifestations, where artificiality is not the premium but naturalness is. Maybe, as science and technology develop and mold the man in the East, life in the East, too, will be similarly conditioned, but there is still a recognition in the East, that the gains of science and technology are double-edged and that it is possible to use them without destroying the beneficient and joyous aspects of our natural, fresh, and elemental urges of life. In summary, the quality of life of a Western individual is at best, and often, only second hand and an imitation of the original.

The man in the West also presents a picture of harboring an elemental violence deep down in his nature. I am not referring here to violence in war, but violence in one's basic make-up in times of peace and security, a violence that is supressed with effort and is not given vent to because of external restraint and which shows tendency of breaking up as soon as the restraints are lifted even in family and loving surroundings. The Westerner gives the impression of, as if it were, itching to be violent on the slightest provocation and perhaps regards it as an enforced limitation that he cannot give vent to his violent reactions. The man from the East, especially India, presents a different picture, in the sense that any violent reaction on his part is not merely the loosening of external restraints but is regarded as a sort of pathology in his nature. An Easterner is by nature more accepting of whatever comes without a similar violent reaction on his own part. The individual in the West is not so integral in his personality as is his counterpart in the East.

The individual in the West can be classed as belonging to an empirically cognitive or reflective category from which corner alone he draws all his sustenance. His intellection alone provides him all his reasons for his action or inaction, feelings, and emotions, as contrasted to a picture of an integrated man who is a whole, a harmony of intellect, feeling, and will, and not intellection alone. This picture is found more frequently in the East or in India than in the West. The personality of an Easterner is not as split, full of discords, disharmonies, and unresolved conflicts within as that of an individual from the West. In fact, the East stresses more the concept of self-realization than knowing.

Instead of a massive array of religious books, pamphlets, periodicals, societies, organizations, church buildings and church going, it seems that the Eastern man, the Indian in particular, whether rich or poor, literate or illiterate, even today lives his life dominated by a sense of the religious or the spiritual. Maybe, in the course of time, this may be lost, but the difference in the lives and pictures of man in the East and in the West is still seen when considered from this point of view. What is meant here by a sense of the religious is not the externals of the religions or the observances of the rituals, etc., but that the peculiar, loving, unruffled sense of service and kindness to all in daily life is identical or same in the different religions of the world.

Deep down in his soul, the image that an Easterner produces in keenly observant minds is his theocratic response and behavior which are almost exclusively determined by his religion or idea of the sacred, which remains a structure of his fundamental consciousness. Not that the picture is never to be found in the West, but the Easterner is inclined to think that the West has at best a second-hand religion, the object of which is merely the intellectual acceptance of doctrinal orthodoxy rather than a spiritual experience. An Easterner is more easily able to hold together and reconcile a variety and multiplicity of views and contradictions without hesitation and difficulty than is a Westerner who is more cut and dried, that is, either this or that, truth or untruth, friend or foe.

To the Easterner, there is no law greater than the law of continuity, wherein opposites are merely differences of degree and not differences of quality. There are no strict dichotomies, especially in the mind of an Indian. Even materialism is not exclusively banished from the spiritual field. God is alternatively what the individual sees in Him. The Divine also has infinite levels. The Eastern man gives a picture of syncretism in his make-up, in all kinds of situations and in doctrine, thought, and practice. If you ask me whether I am a Hindu or Christian, I find it difficult to reply. I am a Hindu because I was born in that particular family.

As a result, the man in the West produces a picture of more strife and stress, pressure, and strain than does the man in the East. This is not to say that the man in the West is merely more industrious and hardworking but to say that, in addition, he is, in some undesirable sense, more than merely hardworking. This need not be. Western man presents a different picture when he is relaxed than when he is at work. The end-all and the be-all of his life is success, no matter where. On the contrary, the man in the East presents a picture of following some ideal unmindful of success or failure and this is one reason why he does not need as much relaxation as his counterpart in the West, because in a deeper sense, he is always relaxed even in the midst of work.

We have to admit that the individual in the East or in the West is not perfect, and it would be just as foolish or unfair to condemn either one. There are obvious difficulties in the evaluation of either the Eastern or the Western man, but we need not go into these difficulties here, except to admit that the present task cannot free us from doubt and has no claim to any finality. There is a tendency in all of us, Eastern or Western, to regard ourselves and the group we belong to as superior to any other. Asia or the East is also changing, and the distinctions drawn between the Easterner and the Westerner will have to be re-evaluated in the course of time. There may soon come an age of industrialization in the East with attendant changes in the familial and social relationships. Many of the features that differentiate traditional Asia from the West may no longer remain uniquely Asian. Eventually, we will have to drop the terms Orient and Occident, except to indicate geographical locations.

It appears that an Easterner differs from his Western counterpart in the concept of the family. To a Westerner, his family means only his wife and children. That is to say, he understands family as a two-generation concept, himself and his children, occasionally perhaps including a third generation, his parents. Family in the

East is a multi-generation concept. It at least includes within it, besides one's wife and children, one's own parents, the parents of one's parents, along with the numerous relations by marriage. It is bewildering to a Westerner how smoothness and solidarity could at all be claimed in an Eastern family, but family solidarity is a fact even today, though changes are coming in the East because of the industrial and urbanizing forces of life.

A Westerner, by and large, is a product of natural and human conditions which determine his values and ideals. He is in his own being a three-dimensional personality. The social and the legal norms and regulations of his time exhaust his universe. Not so with an Eastern individual, for whom the social, the legal, and the human world is a purely man-made universe, smaller and only an observable part of the universe which does not wholly determine his entire being. He is always a part of a dual universe, the man-made universe and an over-man universe, which is neither man-made nor nature-made, and he accepts both in some ways. He accepts and recognizes his subservience to both the smaller and the bigger universe. This permeates his life in all its spheres, and explains why he is so tolerant of religious differences and does not know of the religious persecution the West has known. The Eastern individual is more synthetic and believes in and tolerates the multitude of different behaviors on the part of men belonging to the vast universe. He has a half-believing mentality towards all possibilities, predictions, and miracles.

The Eastern man has an attitude toward the animal world that is not shared by the Western man. The Indian is a respecter of all living beings, however low. He is reluctant to regard the animal kingdom as a means for the sustenance of man. Non-killing of animals is the greatest virtue. He believes that no living animal likes to be killed and that they also feel hurt just as much as human beings. He, therefore, avoids hurting animals and practices what is called "Ahimsa," or non-hurting of living beings, at least in the matter of his pride in slaughtering and killing animals for his dietary pleasures and palate.

The above may appear to the readers as too flattering an image of the Eastern individual. But this is not the intention of the author. This essay is not meant to be evaluatory. The idea is simply to put into words the aspects in which individuals from the two hemispheres seem to differ. To be sure, the East suffers from innumerable evils from which the West has in the course of time freed itself, but the present evils of the East are all automatically remedied by the spread of a liberal, scientific, and technological education. Hence, mention has been made only of the deeper conditions of man both in the East and the West. The author may be totally wrong in what has been depicted and wishes to apologize to anyone who has been offended. After all, this chapter is a personal and impressionistic portrayal which is open to revision, further reflection, and understanding. The author does not claim to understand the Western man as well as he would have liked to.

PB-7811-14-SB
5-05